Winning Against Foreclosure

**Lenders are using foreclosures to steal us blind.
Uncover their game plan and learn how to win!**

BY

RICHARD MERRILL KAHN

http://www.WinningAgainstForeclosure.com

Forensic Professionals Group USA, Inc.

http://www.FPG-USA.com
"Mortgage Analysis as part of a Credible Defense Against Foreclosure"
Serving all 50 States

Winning Against Foreclosure

Published by
Forensic Professionals Group USA, Inc.
http://www.FPG-USA.com

ISBN: 978-0-615-29688-3

Manufactured in the United States of America

About the Author

Richard Kahn has had a professional career in mortgage analysis, residential and commercial real estate, mortgage backed securities and lender financing that has spanned more than thirty years and billions of dollars in equity and mortgages. He has extensive experience in courts including County, State (from Circuit to Supreme), and Federal (from District to Appeals) including Federal Bankruptcy and Appeals. He is FPG-USA's qualifying expert witness on all FPG-USA issuances. Mr. Kahn has held licenses in securities, real estate, and mortgage finance.

EXPERIENCE

1973 through 1977: Richard Kahn began his professional career on Wall Street for Merrill Lynch. There he was involved with one of C.E.O. Donald Regan's projects, appointed in the capacity of National Real Estate Tax Shelter Product Manager of Merrill Lynch. (This is the same Mr. Regan who went on in 1981 to become the 66th United States Treasury Secretary in President Ronald Reagan's Administration.) While at Merrill Lynch, Mr. Kahn analyzed, structured and handled billions of dollars in mortgage backed securities and syndicated real estate investments across Merrill's base of six thousand account executives.

1978 through 1994: Mr. Kahn was C.E.O. and a founding partner of Affiliated Real Estate Analysts (AREA). At AREA, Mr. Kahn personally analyzed over one billion dollars of securitized mortgage backed securities, real estate transactions, mortgage financing, lender compliance analysis and forensic discovery.

1995 through 2005: Mr. Kahn was C.E.O. and a founding partner of Mallpark, Inc. Mallpark was a cutting edge internet and online presence provider specializing in secure protocols and merchant processing. At its peak, Mallpark provided services to over 500,000 individual online merchants.

1995 through 2008: Mr. Kahn was principal broker and partner of various real estate, mortgage brokerage and lending institutions. His skills in real estate and mortgage analysis established a track record of hundreds of millions of dollars in business without one compliance violation, complaint or bad loan buy back.

2008 through Present: Mr. Kahn is C.E.O., and Founding partner of Forensic Professionals Group USA, Inc. (FPG-USA). He is co-creator and co-inventor of FPG-USA's patent pending online automated Lender Compliance Analysis and Forensic Lender Discovery systems. He is a working partner, a director and the supervising senior mortgage analyst. He is the qualifying witness on issuances in the process of submission into evidence in all Courts, in all States

Court Experience

Mr. Kahn has personally been involved in securitized mortgage backed securities, real estate, mortgage finance and taxation; analysis, reporting, litigation, negotiation and settlement. He has appeared in State and Federal courts including both civil process and Bankruptcy process. He has been deposed, interviewed, and questioned innumerable times. He has facilitated hundreds of millions of dollars in workouts with real estate syndicated partnerships, lenders, property owners, mortgage holders, borrowers and government agencies including the Internal Revenue Service and the Justice Department.

PROFESSIONAL LICENSES HELD

FL Correspondent Mortgage Lender Licensing 2004-2009
FL Mortgage Broker: Initial license 1995.Status: Current;
FL. Real Estate Broker Initial 1995. Status Current
NY Real Estate Broker Initial 1986 Status: Expired
Series 7 SEC NYSE NASD Securities Initial 1974. Last 1995

Author's Acknowledgement

I would like to thank my wife Charo and my two youngest children Rebecca and Craig, still living at home, for their enduring patience, support and encouragement during the four months it took to write this book. My wife Charo believes a man is fulfilled when he has children, has planted a tree and authored a book of meaningful value to others. With this book I have accomplished all three.

I would like to thank my oldest daughter Jenna for her interest, taking the time to read the initial work and providing initial editing and opinion.

I would especially like to thank my FPG-USA business partner and long time friend Paul Holzmann. Paul believed the topic was important and allowed me the time during four months to create it, encouraging me all the way. Most of all I'd like to thank Paul for his in-depth interest in all aspects of the book and the many long and challenging hours he spent editing the entire work from its original form to what is being published today. I handed Paul a 570 page author's first work. In cutting half of the book away, Paul has trimmed the fat and left only the meat.

I would also like to thank Erika Holzmann, Paul's lovely wife and Helen, his daughter for allowing Paul to spend many hours that would otherwise have been devoted to the family working on this book.

Table of Contents

Introduction

Burn me once shame on you, burn me twice, shame on me. Borrowers, attorneys fighting foreclosure, and others in the mix that did not do their homework, research and investigation, or hire experts to do this for them are losing the fight against foreclosure right now, today.

Even in the face of losing, they are saying they "get it", when they simply don't.

One of the most frustrating things about this phenomenon is seeing experts speak on the news, on blogs, and television and profess their understanding of the problem and its solutions, when most really don't have a clue. This is evidenced by the fact that they do not offer the solutions to solve the problems and they do not teach people facing foreclosure from predatory lenders how to win.

Why are we not hearing the immediate solutions for the millions facing foreclosure being blasted from every roof top in the land? What are those solutions?

This book lays it out for you in black and white. Embarking on this journey of understanding will reveal it all for borrowers, attorneys, media, politicians, judges, government, and others to finally understand how we got here, what we are up against, and how to win the battle against the predatory lenders.

Part One
History and Background

The foreclosure debacle confronting borrowers today precipitated the Meltdown of 2008. This was caused by the securitization of predatory mortgage loans originated between the years 2000 and 2007 that were destined to default in mass.

Securitization begins with the pooling together of individual mortgages into billion dollar packages which are then marked up and sold to unwitting Wall Street investors.

The process involves the cooperation of non regulated mortgage lenders (hereafter "NRM Lenders"), Wall Street Investment Banking firms and International Banking firm Trustees representing the investors.

Capitalizing on many years of selling good loan securitization programs to investors, the NRM Lenders deceptively sold predatory loans designed to default, to unwitting borrowers as good loans

The NRM Lenders have created a plan to profit through foreclosure and capitalize on the public's perception that the lender is losing money in this process. Surprisingly, the opposite is true; the NRM Lenders are winning extravagantly in the process. The losers are the borrower and the investor.

To understand this uncommon process one must go back to the time leading up to the Great Depression when the NRM Lenders of that day used the same tactics to cause the Great Depression. Franklin Roosevelt and his Congress fixed the problems and restricted these NRM Lenders from operating on Wall Street. This protected borrowers until November 1999 when Bill Clinton's Republican Congress repealed the critical Banking Act of 1933 which had protected Americans since its passage, and opened the door to the Meltdown of 2008.

To fight foreclosure today is relatively easy if you look at the past. The intent of the following chapters is to help the reader build a new understanding of how the current situation came about, how to solve the problems, and how to prevent this type of situation from happening again and most importantly of all, provide a foundation of knowledge to initiate the process of winning against foreclosure.

Chapter 1

Our History of Predatory Lending

Thomas Jefferson warned us in 1802. "I believe that banking institutions are more dangerous to our liberties than standing armies. If the American people ever allow private banks to control the issue of their currency, first by inflation, then by deflation, the banks and corporations that will grow up around [the banks] will deprive the people of all property until their children wake-up homeless on the continent their fathers conquered."

As a result of the Mortgage Meltdown of 2008, borrowers, their attorneys, and loan modification professionals are now battling banks in courts around the country to try to prevent the homelessness that Jefferson predicted. Borrowers' attorneys are desperately seeking credible defenses against lenders, who talk about modifying loans, but are instead, barreling down the legal road to foreclosure.

This book is designed to help those attorneys and loan modification professionals assisting these borrowers. The sad fact is that many attorneys are new to this area of law and do not understand the enemy or the methods and processes necessary to beat them. They are Babes in the Wood. This book will show how to beat the non regulated mortgage (NRM) lenders who issued predatory loans to borrowers by using two simple weapons, Lender Compliance Analysis [SM] and Forensic Lender Discovery [SM]. These tools can also greatly assist in negotiating a loan modification and settlement from a position of strength.

Predatory Lending and Ruthless Profiteering is well documented in American history. Because of this, Congress has legislated and protected borrowers against the wrongs of unfair, abusive, and deceptive lending.

Now Vs. Then
Let's take a look at history to see how the same general lender strategy, albeit with far less complexity, was used to similar ends by non regulated mortgage lenders in the Great Depression Era.

Nearly the same set of circumstances that we are experiencing today (Now) happened during that time (Then).

In Both Times:

1. The Non Regulated Mortgage (NRM) Lenders were at the core of the problems.
2. The same type of mortgage crisis and manipulated stock, bond, and securities markets occurred.
3. The same inside information was used to earn incredible fortunes by NRM Lenders who could reliably predict when the bottom would fall out of the stock and bond markets due to predictable toxic default of underlying mortgages.
4. The resulting consolidations among corporate giants was monumental and the profiteering immense. Big banks, giant investment houses, and monolithic (at one time in the past) corporations were sucked up, absorbed and repositioned in the frenzy.
5. The masses were told the same lies leading up to the crisis: Banks do not want to foreclose. Yet millions upon millions of people were made homeless because the banks *did* foreclose. An action that speaks louder than words.

Then:

1. There were billions of dollars raised, not trillions.
2. Borrowers did not have the same consumer welfare programs available now.

Now:

1. NRM Lenders and their co-conspirator Investment Banking partners sold sophisticated investment vehicles and stocks at the highest prices, only to buy them back a short time later for pennies on the dollar. Because of this, there were trillions of dollars raised globally for even more drastic profits.
2. Borrowers have consumer welfare programs. Although these may be a saving grace for some citizens, they are also an additional drain on taxpayer wallets and government coffers.

At the end of the Great Depression, Congress, under Franklin D. Roosevelt, passed the Banking Act of 1933 which stopped the NRM Lenders from teaming up with securities firms, thereby protecting borrowers. About half a century later, with the lessons learned in the Great Depression forgotten, the NRM Lenders began lobbying to get into the Securities business. Finally, in November 1999, the Banking Act of 1933 was repealed. This was outgoing President Bill Clinton's Republican Congress's gift to the incoming President George W. Bush's new administration. It was to be a legacy of financial disaster that would materialize itself in the meltdown of 2008.

After winning repeal of the Banking Act in November 1999, the NRM Lenders exploded out of the gate in January 2000. They kept running until the Meltdown in 2008. They have now switched gears to foreclosure and are up and running again. Today, NRM Lenders have successfully mobilized their front line warriors, the National Servicing Platforms' Foreclosure Mill attorneys, to do battle against borrowers facing foreclosure.

Masses of attorneys are rallying to try to successfully represent the borrowers who are under attack. Unfortunately, far too many attorneys have only just recently entered this realm of foreclosure defense and have no real strategy to do battle against the NRM Lenders. The influx of non-seasoned attorneys into foreclosure defense may be attributed to a combination of issues. The dramatic rise in foreclosures triggered by the Meltdown of 2008, the slowdown of real estate closings, and the drop in immigration[1] are just a few. There is no denying the massive need for foreclosure defense. It is the few, not the many, who have been doing bankruptcy and foreclosure defense for decades and have helped thousands of consumers. It is now time for the few to step up and help the many learn to fight foreclosure with proven methods to produce good long term loan modification settlements to save the home or sell it.

The NRM Lenders are counting on this new breed of foreclosure defense attorneys not being able to mount formidable defenses in time to save their clients. As the dust settles, the foreclosed properties are winding up owned by the NRM Lenders in REO (real estate owned) portfolios. The NRM Lenders are trickling these properties out slowly, so as not to flood the market. Over the coming years, this strategy is planned to produce phenomenal profits on the backs of the phenomenal losses suffered by borrowers in foreclosure.

Nothing in the new foreclosure defense attorneys' past careers has prepared them for this type of battle. It appears that the legal and court systems are playing right into the hands of the NRM Lenders, by thinking of these foreclosures as "traditional mortgages" gone bad, where a lender gives a loan, has risk in it, and services it (or uses third party loan servicing). They don't realize that in reality borrowers are losing their homes to predatory lenders who issued deceptive loans designed to default, strip the equity from the borrower, and deliver the homes in foreclosure to the lender who has already been paid in full on the mortgage and has no risk whatsoever in the loan itself. Miraculously, this is being done while the lender is profiting extraordinarily while in the process of crying wolf and claiming losses. The relative handful of judges and attorneys who do understand are making a difference. However, due to the sheer numbers of existing foreclosures and new foreclosures coming online every day, it is a drop in the bucket. While one or two borrowers are being saved, thousands upon thousands are losing their homes to foreclosure. The information this book offers is meant to join the existing effort to save borrowers and educate their attorneys and loan modification

---

[1] Immigration slows as downturn bites: study. Reuters Jan 14, 2009 by Tim Gaynor

professionals. Congress has empowered borrowers to fight foreclosure using consumer protection acts in existence today.

Consumer Protection Act violations and remedies are the Achilles Heel of the NRM Lenders.

Starting in the Great Depression, congress legislated massive consumer protections via numerous government agencies designed to fight against the unscrupulous predatory banks and investment securities firms. These consumer protections include The Truth in Lending Act (TILA) ; the Real Estate and Settlement Procedures Act (RESPA); the Home Ownership and Equity Protection Act (HOEPA); and finally, the Federal Trade Commission Act (FTC Act section 45) against Unfair and Deceptive Acts and Practices (UDAP) which also serves as a model for State consumer protection laws. Unfortunately, the single most important of these NRM Lender limiting actions was the Banking Act of 1933 which was repealed 1999.

This book will explain the two weapons (Lender Compliance Analysis [SM] and Forensic Lender Discovery [SM]), that can provide the necessary leverage to take advantage of the consumer protection acts mentioned above and exploit the NRM Lenders' Achilles Heels, in order to Win Against Foreclosure.

Chapter 2

National Mortgage Servicing Platforms

The borrower is not up against traditional lending, by any means. Many readers may not even be aware that the National Mortgage Servicing Platforms (NMSP) exist. This is somewhat remarkable considering the size and prevalence of their involvement supporting the NRM Lender operations and securitization.

On the surface, mortgage banking and securities operations include:
- Pooling mortgages together and selling them to investors
- the Wall Street investment banking aspect
- Managing the securities administration and investor's aspect
- Daily "performing" borrower loan servicing operations
- In house borrower and investor side legal departments
- Borrower default servicing collection departments
- Attorneys pursuing borrower foreclosure actions

There are additional players behind the NRM Lenders. These "behind the scenes" operations are more commonly referred to as "National Mortgage Servicing Platforms" (NMSP). They supply and control all the talent necessary for all of the NRM Lenders' needs, nicely stacked in comprehensive vertical corporations and their subsidiaries that broadly fall into three categories:
- Information Service Providers
- Default Solutions Service Providers
- Foreclosure mills

These giant National Mortgage Servicing Platforms are the "brains and brawn" behind the NRM Lending operations. They can:

- manage the origination side of pooling the mortgages
- facilitate all aspects of securitization
- package the product for Wall Street
- make sure the obligations to investors are met
- facilitate essential loan servicing operations
- facilitate the in house legal departments of servicing lenders
- perform default loan servicing and collections
- provide lender foreclosure legal services
- operate the lender's REO (Real Estate Owned) side of the foreclosures

Considering the breadth and magnitude of these National Mortgage Servicing Platform operations, it's quite impressive that they operate in the background, out of the public eye. It is not uncommon to find people in the industry that have no clue about the existence of the NMSP Operations. On the servicing lender side, loss mitigation personnel may not be aware of how the operations run within their own firm.

NRM Lender's utilize powerful legal foreclosure mills. These foreclosure mills are actually independent law firms that have morphed into huge foreclosure case assembly lines pumping out several thousand new foreclosures a month. The foreclosure mills are judged by the Default Servicing Platforms that hand out new cases on the basis of speed in accomplishing foreclosure. The faster that the borrowers are brought to foreclosure, the more cases the foreclosure mill receives each month. This mass assembly line process has an inherent sloppiness factor due to handling gigantic amounts of new and existing case loads. Don't imagine the hard working lawyer burning the midnight oil and toiling with a particular lender's case day and night. Not even close. These attorneys and paralegals are working hard, but on colossal numbers of different foreclosure case files. They are deeply pitted against the borrowers in foreclosure. Many of the individual attorneys earn more working there than they would elsewhere, considering their experience. They open and shut their cases quickly and make fortunes in the process.

Chapter 3

The Entire Scheme Is Built On Predatory Loan Programs

Wall Street investment bankers were excited over the monumental win-win-win opportunity of bringing investors into high quality transactions that would pay huge commissions and fees to the account executives and investment firms, satisfy the NRM Lenders who were originating the loans and provide good loans to borrowers. The combination of above average predictable income, broad borrower bases, high Credit Ratings Agency (Standard & Poor's, Moody's and Fitch) ratings and strong capital appreciation from paying down mortgages over time, were an alluring combination.

Most exciting though, were the staggering trillions of investor dollar amounts out there for the taking. With typical transactions in the billion and half billion dollar range, the commissions and fees would also be staggering. In the 1970's and 1980's, large transactions were in the tens of millions and hundreds of millions. In the marketplace of the NRM Lenders running from 2000 to the Meltdown in 2008, single transaction amounts were in the billion dollar range!

One can only imagine how this made Wall Street salivate. All Wall Street had to do was supply the investors and investment banks as Trustees. That was easy. The NRM Lenders would provide the product, service, and support. Wall Street would do the selling, for which they would be paid handsomely. The Wall Street investment firms would also have the opportunity to earn vast sums from insider partnerships and co-ventures that would not be readily apparent, but covered in the disclosures to protect all. These hidden areas are covered in detail in the diagram and key notes sections of this book.

The question of supply of mortgages to meet the demand was answered with "creative" predatory loan programs. The NRM Lenders would take care of the borrower side of the equation. The National Servicing Platforms would handle logistics between all parties.

The challenge for NRM Lenders was supplying enough mortgages for the loan pool demand. There were many trillions more investor dollars for high grade mortgage pools than there were high grade credit borrowers with residential mortgages. Sensible companies would sell only those credit grade borrower mortgages that fit the quality requirements. NRM Lenders could not pass up the trillions of dollars of investor pool monies available, so they created what for them was a better solution. New mortgage terms that would inspire everyone to refinance in what the borrowers believed were good mortgages but instead, turned out to be toxic predatory mortgages designed to default. The ruse would receive strong government backing. State government coffers would be enriched from the transfer and note taxes on each new mortgage transaction. The federal government would easily be lobbied with increased state tax revenue, because States would now seek less financial assistance from the Federal Government.

Wall Street investment firms were responsible for organizing the investor documentation and disclosures in compliance with Securities and Exchange Commission (SEC) disclosure rules. On average, typical investor documentation involved many hundreds and often over a thousand pages combined in each separate transaction. This meant tremendous fees to participating law firms, accounting firms, and interim parties.

On the investor side, the documentation strategy was simple. It would be crushing in its magnitude of small print and cross referenced legalese. Account executives would use relationships and reliance on trust and long term business strategies to instill confidence.

Wall Street relied on the previous years of sensible bank originated mortgage backed securitized transactions that didn't cause meltdowns.

This history would serve as an example of returns investors could look forward to. Banks had been successfully financing pools of properties in "real deals" for years. The problem was, those real deals often involved the investors owning the properties and actually being the borrowers. In that way, they could earn cash flows as well as earn equity over the years as the mortgages were paid off by the rents. The target of equity by the originators in those real deals typically came after the investors earned an agreed to percentage. For example, over a certain amount the originators earned 30% and the investors 70%.

In the new transactions, to gain equity, the originators would have to resort to more sinister means. The simple solution would put NRM Lender interests at opposite sides of the investors in securitized pools, but full disclosure would protect the actions. It would require issuing loans destined to foreclose on the borrower side, and being awarded the home in foreclosure through the loan servicer on the investor side. This could only be done by cross collateralizing the investor in such a way that the investors would think they were insured against loses. The NRM Lenders would allege that foreclosure costs far more than it does and is a far more burdensome process than it is, and rely on traditional lending interpretations to uphold those claims.

In reality, the foreclosure process was relatively inexpensive in comparison to the windfall profits of a home received free and clear in foreclosure because the original mortgage was paid in full by the investors from day one. Paperwork in the pooling and servicing agreements would provide that the servicers receive all payments owed from a foreclosure process.

The securitization process required pooling mortgages together. Therefore, the loan programs underlying the pools were of paramount importance. Unfortunately after the repeal of the Banking Act of 1933, the predatory non regulated mortgage lenders got back into the game. Their model was the same that was used by the Great Depression era banks in that it used extremely risky (to the borrower) loan products such as interest only loans to take in business. It also included foreclosure and stock market securities manipulation.

What could give the NRM Lenders the ability to attract borrowers to refinance and make purchases? Super low "teaser" interest rates promised for a predictable period that would fit into a marketing plan to capture all the mortgage origination over say, six years (2000 to 2006). These seemingly cheap mortgages would spur real estate purchases and fuel rising real estate values, as interest only loans did back in the Great Depression Era. This could not be avoided, so the NRM Lenders also had to create a plan to capture the financial benefits of that phenomenon. NRM Lenders would use the same strategy as their predecessor predatory lenders in the 1930's: Massive foreclosures.

The strategy required developing loan programs that were toxic in their very nature while seeming to be feasible. Here is an example:

To implement the plan of foreclosure, the super low teaser interest rates might not be enough to pay the interest only portion due each month. To allow this, the unpaid difference would be tacked onto the principal amount in a method called negative amortization. The plan would allow varying maximum increases in the principal from about 110% of the mortgage up to about 125% of the mortgage. This was called the "recast" rate. For instance, in a 125% plan, the low teaser rate could be paid in the form or a payment option, called a "minimum payment" until the mortgage increased to the recast rate of 125%, at which point the minimum payment option would no longer be available and only the fully amortizing rate based on the balance of years left on the mortgage could be paid. This recast caused mortgage payments to skyrocket overnight and triggered massive defaults by borrowers who could not make the payments.

To make matters much worse, when real estate values stopped appreciating, borrowers would not be able to refinance. The mortgage would then be "upside down" which is when the outstanding mortgage amount exceeds the value of the property. This exacerbated the problem for the borrowers because the homes would not qualify for refinance loans, which required some amount of borrower equity to be in place. Borrowers would not be able to afford the new payments and the properties could not be refinanced. Foreclosure would sweep the land. From the NRM Lender's point of view, that was perfect.

In public, the NRM Lenders would cry painfully that they were suffering due to foreclosures because people at large understood traditional banking. Everyone would believe the NRM Lenders were losing money. But in private, the NRM Lenders knew they would be paid in full within days of selling the mortgages to the investor at the beginning of the mortgage pool transaction. So, in reality, the NRM Lenders didn't have one thin dime of risk in the mortgages. By the time the general public and legal system figured out what was really happening it would be too late. NRM Lenders would own millions upon millions of American citizens' homes via foreclosure.

There was a lot riding on the terms the NRM Lenders needed to create in the new mortgages in order to accomplish their goals.

NRM Lenders developed products with program highlights such as:
- ARMs – Adjustable Rate Mortgages,
- Neg-Ams – Negatively Amortizing Mortgages,
- Adjusting
- Recasting

Borrowers had no idea that these seemingly fantastic new programs would turn borrowers into victims at a predictable point in time.

The NRM Lender plan also encompassed new underwriting phenomena to achieve more mortgage "product" to meet investor demand.
- No income No Asset
- Stated Income No Asset
- No Income Stated Asset
- Stated Income Stated Asset

The age old benchmarks of a successful loan transaction were set aside. Income, length of employment and savings would not be verified in the traditional sense. NRM Lenders instead would accept borrower income and asset verification that was stated or not checked at all.

NRM Lenders designed the payments based on a ridiculously low start rate such as one or two percent. This would mask the eight or nine percent actually being charged to subprime borrowers, at least for a certain period of time. Call it two, three, or even five years; long enough to sell more products to Wall Street investors before the loans began defaulting in bulk. By adding unpaid interest each month to the outstanding principal balance in the form of negative amortization, the amount owed would quickly escalate and in most cases, the only viable option when the mortgage payment adjusted to the full nominal note rate was foreclosure. That fit perfectly into the NRM Lenders plan.

NRM Lenders had additional challenges. Even if they gave mortgages to everyone and anyone, there were still trillions upon trillions more dollars out there from investors. Since the window of opportunity was only going to be six or seven years, the problem of capturing all that money also required creating a new investment vehicle. These were labeled Collateralized Debt Obligations (CDOs). Through these CDOs, mortgages could be sold and resold many times. The problem would be transferring the note and mortgage. For this purpose the NRM Lenders created MERS, the Mortgage Electronic Registration System. This will be covered in detail in the chapter on MERS.

In the aftermath of the Meltdown of 2008, it has become painfully obvious that many borrowers did not understand the loan products they signed their names to. Additionally, in many instances, the underwriting standards proved so lax that loans were issued to borrowers who did not sign the documentation themselves, or were based on completely fictitious documentation entirely. The NRM Lenders didn't care. As soon as they originated the mortgages and sold them to investors, they were paid in full and more.

The entire scheme revolved around creating loan terms and programs that would satisfy the appearance of being in the best interest of the borrower when in fact, they were in the best interest of the NRM Lender. After making all the profit in the securitization process, the NRM Lenders would then affect their exit strategy of acquiring the properties in foreclosure. This separation would resolve the potential liability they faced from unhappy investors seeking to sue them in court. There were a number of critical mortgage terms at the root of the problem.

ARMs – Adjustable Rate Mortgages
This example will use simple numbers rounded off to the nearest $100. By using an ARM that is fixed for a certain period (say 1, 2, 3 or 5 years for example), a borrower could lower the payment on a $250,000 mortgage to around $1,000 on a 5% Interest Only ARM; vs. $1,800 at 8% fixed for 30 years. That's a big difference, especially when taxes and insurance are also added to the picture.

Minimum Payment Option ARMS
Using the above ARM example, with the minimum payment option touched on earlier in this chapter, the mortgage payment could be brought down even further. The $250,000 mortgage at a 1% minimum payment would be $800 vs. $1,800. The difference is added each month to the mortgage principal amount under negative amortization.

Neg-Am – Negative Amortization
The nefarious Neg-Am feature can really attract borrowers with teaser rates as low as 1% to 1.5% principle and interest. See the example immediately above. Neg-Am loans are actually very simple to understand. Whatever amount is not paid under the regular interest rate calculation is added to the principal amount of the mortgage. In concert with the lower teaser rate, the principal amount of a $300,000 mortgage could rise to between $330,000 and $375,000 in a few years time, or less.

Recast Limit
This is a limit to which principal in a neg-am mortgage can be added before the loan is recalculated. Recast is usually a percent expressed as 110%, 115%, 120% and 125%. This is how the rise in principle (above) is calculated. 110% represents the $330,000 up to the 25% which represents the $375,000.

Recast Adjustment
At the point the mortgage hit its maximum recast limit, the loan must be recalculated to a fixed rate mortgage at the fully indexed nominal note rate (for example 8% on a subprime loan) and the amortization, the period the loan was paid down to zero would be the years

remaining. In a thirty year mortgage that has been paid for three years, the amortization period would be twenty seven years.

Using simple round off math, look at the results of a neg-am loan recasting. For this example, use a 30 year loan of $250,000 with a recast limit of 125%. The loan reaches its maximum limit after two or so years at the 1.5% start rate which provided a very affordable $862 monthly payment. The new principal amount is $312,500 and the fully indexed nominal note rate is 8%. The new payment is $2300 fixed per month for 28 years. That's over a $1,400 increase over the $862 per month the borrower had been paying prior to the recast.

Additionally, loan refinances for borrowers in this position are nearly impossible unless the real estate market has climbed faster than the neg-am rate. An unlikely scenario, especially considering only 90% or less can be refinanced, not the full 100% that can be financed on a purchase.

Now enter recast deception to make things even worse.

Recast Deception
Recasting is an onerous event. Payments spike overnight and in most cases, refinancing is impossible. Without going into the mathematical calculations and complications, most recast deception occurs in the Truth in Lending Disclosure Payment Schedule. The lowest payment is projected to the limit of years allowed. So the borrower sees the lowest payment and also sees the longest number of years. The truth of the matter is that if calculations are performed based on a borrower making only minimum payments and the loan recasts before the projected recast period on the payment schedule, there is a critical violation of TILA. For example, the minimum payment shows $1,000 per month for five years on the payment schedule. But if the minimum payment of $1,000 is made every month and the loan recasts in three years, then this is deception according to TILA.

20

Upside Down
This is where the outstanding mortgage amount is more than the property is worth when closing costs and expenses to sell or refinance are factored in. For example, the $250,000 mortgage referred to above that negatively amortizes to $312,500 was originally taken on a property sold for $317,000. Unfortunately, the market value has fallen and the home is now only worth $250,000. The property is now, by definition, upside down. Refinance is impossible. Either the borrower pays the higher mortgage payment or the banks will foreclosure.

No pulse, no problem.
The NRM Lenders, like all lenders, developed ongoing programs to teach their loan officers and mortgage brokers how to sell what amounts to over a trillion dollars in loans. These same loan officers and brokers trained by the NRM Lenders were served up as those responsible for the abuses on borrowers. Whoever is to blame, the loans were accomplished. No income, no problem. No assets, no problem. No employer verification, no problem. No pulse, hmmm... okay we'll do it in someone else's name - no problem!

The method to lure borrowers to default on their mortgages was created. The NRM Lenders would capitalize on the window of opportunity before it closed and defaults started to pour in. With the plan set and viable, the NRM Lenders and their securities investment banking counterparts now had no time to waste. The rush to securitization was on.

Chapter 4

Manipulating Borrowers Trust for Gain

It is appropriate to touch on the borrowers' and brokers' trust being captured and then violated.

The NRM Lenders' strategy was extraordinarily simple. Send the mortgage brokers out with new loan programs designed to fail but advertised as being totally legitimate. Then, instead of protecting the brokers when the mortgages fail, hang them out to dry.

Lenders have always wanted to get the mortgage broker middleman out of the picture because the brokers drained off too much profit and they were always open to the greed of a quick buck. This would be the brokers' downfall.

Borrowers trusted the mortgage brokers. Borrowers never understood the hidden rebates lenders paid to the mortgage brokers in the form of yield spread premiums, par plus, and lender paid broker commission, etc. Borrowers didn't understand that these fees paid to brokers, were raised by increasing the interest rate on the loan. HUD settlement statements carried this small print disclosure outside of the regular column structure. Broker agreements did the same or couched the fees in percentages instead of raw numbers, or if raw numbers were provided, it was done in such a way that they could easily be passed over.

In reality, brokers never risk their own money. They represent the lender products for a commission. Borrowers can be charged commissions, which is normally the case in a brokered transaction.

When this is added to the hidden lender paid broker commissions, mortgage brokers could make four and five percentage points on a loan.

A three hundred thousand dollar loan could pay a mortgage broker fifteen thousand dollars per loan. Greed and the ability to play "disclosure sleight of hand" created the perfect formula for the brokers' demise. Finally, Lenders could be rid of the middleman that got in between their profits and the borrower. They finally accomplished this by laying all the blame or most of the blame at the feet of the mortgage brokers.

The laws of disclosure enable Lenders to avoid divulging their profits in a mortgage. Lenders hoped that the act of requiring disclosure by the brokers of fees earned for brokering, would move borrowers directly to lenders on whose Hud-1 settlement statements little or no brokerage fees were included. Disclosure of mortgage broker fees was originally optimistically thought by lenders to be an impediment to the mortgage brokers' success. This proved not to be the case at all. The government agency regulating settlement procedures and disclosure in this regard under RESPA is HUD, the U.S. Department of Housing and Urban Development. Why the disclosure of broker fees didn't discourage borrowers to use brokers is not fully understood. Perhaps the brokers were too charming or presented their own products in such a way that the borrower didn't mind paying the broker fee. In any event, mortgage brokers maintained a substantial piece of the mortgage loan origination business. This has stood as a thorn in the side of lenders who prefer not to pay middlemen to sell lender products to borrowers.

For the record, in this chapter, the term mortgage broker also includes loan officers.

The NRM Lenders had full control of the paperwork, the NRM Lenders promoted the toxic loan programs to the mortgage brokers with huge financial incentives to push these out to borrowers. The NRM Lenders' loan quality control (QC) checks and balances which were instituted and required to be performed at all levels, didn't simply fail. The NRM Lenders were happy to finance anything and everything, as long as they could get the mortgages to sell and resell over and over again and then wind up with the property via foreclosure in the end.

Who could imagine that the NRM Lender could profit one million dollars on a two hundred fifty thousand dollar loan by selling the same loan over and over in the form of synthetic collateralize debt obligations, with little or no media attention? The question of why so much attention was generated toward the mortgage broker profit may be attributed to excellent NRM Lender media control. The mortgage brokers have been annihilated by the 2008 Meltdown while the NRM Lenders are stealing homes through toxic predatory mortgages made to unsuspecting borrowers. For the lending industry in general, the ancillary benefit of NRM Lenders finally assisting the home run of pushing mortgage brokers out of the picture, is a long awaited triumph for lenders. Pushing the dishonest malleable brokers out serves all, but historically the honest mortgage brokers have served borrowers over the years by shopping across many lenders for the best and most suitable products at the best terms and conditions.

Congress has empowered borrowers' and their attorneys to fight against the NRM Lender seeking to foreclose on predatory loans in violation of government agency rules and regulations. For those attorneys "in the know", simple forensic loan audits and discovery from credible third party evidence can be submitted into court as evidence with predictable violation remedies and results.

One of the problems to surmount is a lack of specific knowledge on this process, which is a target this book seeks to address. The other is on the borrower side, which manifests itself in the lack of trust of borrowers have for anyone they must pay a fee to. This is understandable given their recent experiences with mortgage brokers who sold them a toxic mortgage while getting paid handsomely for it. Hopefully this book will enlighten borrowers to the process required to win against foreclosure and provide a benchmark for the borrower to assess the skills of their attorney or loan modification professional.

It is difficult, if not impossible to evaluate an attorney's abilities and knowledge in this cutting edge business of foreclosure if one does not have a basic understanding of the real issues. Any borrower, who "thinks" they have the ability to go "pro se" (to defend themselves) against the savvy top flight NRM Lender law firms, is most likely committing legal suicide. If as the saying goes, "A man who is his own lawyer has a fool for his client", how much more so for the borrower who is not an expert at the rules of civil procedure and the due process of the law.

In this regard, a borrower reading this book can hopefully learn what to look for in an attorney they seek to hire to fight foreclosure. An attorney can enhance their legal strategy. Loan modification professionals can use the reporting of violations to work on an alternate track to resolution and settle a good term loan modification where one did not exist before. In this manner, the borrower and their advocates can be moving on a dual track of fighting foreclosure and trying to modify the loan.

Chapter 5

Evidence Vs. Hearsay

Understanding what evidence is and how to establish it is critical to the successful deployment of any legal strategy and warrants a brief discussion.

At the crux of the matter are the Rules of Evidence of State and Federal Courts. This is the way the courts and legal system require evidence to be submitted. Allegations, claims made by one party or another, can be submitted freely within the constraints of the Rules of Civil Procedure. However, allegations are not evidence.

Evidence is very powerful. Properly submitted evidence, with expert witness availability, under the rules of evidence can be motioned (requested) for judicial review. Having the judge review the evidence and draw conclusions, which may be acted upon, is a powerful tool.

The opposing side, in this case the NRM Lender, will try to avoid this from happening at all costs. Should this occur, their first line of defense will be to challenge the evidence.

To support the evidence, it is extremely important that the expert witness, if used, brings sufficient experience and knowledge to support the findings. This knowledge and experience, or lack thereof, will become evident during questioning from the judge and opposing parties in the hearing. Hearings can be conducted in person but are often conducted via conference call with the parties because Judges realize the financial restrictions of a borrower facing foreclosure. Judges and opposing counsel are not to be deceived or underestimated.

Assuming they can easily be fast talked or cajoled into accepting someone as an expert who is far from it, is a big mistake. When a judge expects to hear from an expert, the person claiming to be so must meet the judge's criteria or what is submitted as evidence may become merely hearsay instead of evidence, rendering the evidentiary findings and reporting basically worthless. In residential foreclosure, the acceptability of expert status under the Rules of Evidence is usually the at the judge's sole discretion. Extensive experience in the field is the general benchmark.

An example of a qualified expert witness would be a professional who has held some sort of securities licensing, some sort of real estate broker licensing, and some sort of mortgage lending licensing during their career. In obtaining this licensing, they will likely have produced some sort of evidence to their qualifications in addition to their educational achievements. They should also have real world transactional experience in these various fields to back up their academic credentials and they should be extremely well versed in the subjects they will be questioned on. Additionally, they should be part of the ongoing operations of a real estate mortgage analysis company with IRS tax returns supporting documentable sustained revenue in the field. This will help to prove that they have a track record of doing this type of work. Regardless of all of this, the judge will still have the final word on the acceptability of expert status.

Also, having substantial amounts of previous court experience across different courts is important. What use is an expert who has never testified in a court or had a deposition taken in relation to a case involving their mortgage analysis?

One cannot determine what an individual judge will accept as qualifying experience in their court. However access by the Judge to the one claiming to be a qualifying expert witness is critical. Mortgage compliance analysis reporting may simply be worthless if qualifying expert witness access is not provided under the Rules of Evidence of the Court in the case.

Judges "motioned" to conduct phone conference calls with the parties and the expert may agree to do so in foreclosure cases because judges understand and are sensitive to the financial situation of a borrower facing foreclosure and the expense of expert witnesses appearing in person.

The answer then to the question of "what is an expert in court?" seems to be based on the quality of the issuances and evidentiary findings, the resume of the expert, the availability of the expert to the court and the knowledge of the expert in response to the questioning. The attorney submits the reporting and credentials, then waits for a response or challenge of credibility and applicability and takes it from there.

The reason entering mortgage analysis findings of violations and toxicity into evidence is so important is that it shifts the burden of proof to the lender. One of the critical benefits of a borrower's attorney submitting evidence into a case is that it removes the benefit of assumption that the lender has. Instead of the judge assuming the lender's points, issues, allegations, and assumptions are valid, the lender must now prove their side of the case against the evidence submitted.

In the case of Forensic Lender Discovery SM (FLD) (covered in depth in later chapters) or an equivalent service that seeks to find the toxicity in the securitized mortgage transaction to undermine the ability to foreclose as part of a credible legal defense, the findings and discovery requests are designed to shift the burden of proof onto the lender's shoulders. In foreclosure, the initial burden is on the borrower. When a credible third party mortgage analysis firm finds toxicity and compliance violations and these are accepted into court as evidence, the lender now has the burden of response to prove otherwise. When the initial reporting and discovery is done well, the lender finds them self in the position of divulging information that will be used against them in the case, or as the basis of further discovery of evidence that may be damning in court. When a lender's responsive evidence may ultimately be more damaging to the lender's case than they are willing to admit, the lender may want to avoid producing proper answers to discovery at all costs. This often causes the lender to come to the table and settle in order to avoid disclosing harmful evidence. The settlement objective of the borrower's attorney has now been accomplished. The NRM Lender pushed into the position of choosing to avoid providing damning response knows the outcome in court can go very poorly for them. In essence, this forces the lender to consider making a good long term loan modification settlement, assuming that is the borrower's attorney's desired outcome. Lenders receiving discovery requests under court rules of civil procedure have a specified time to respond, for example 60 days. If they do not respond in that time, they may apply to the court for an extension with good reasons. Additional time may be involved in extensions. If the discovery is not returned within by ultimate time provided, the judge might take more aggressive steps and the case would move solidly to favor the borrower. The delaying process has a predictable time depending on the state and court rules of time frames to respond, but in the end, if the intention of the lender is not to respond because the discovery requests are too incriminating, then this time frame is a excellent window of opportunity to effect a good long term loan modification settlement to save or sell. It will not surprise attorneys to find that in many cases, settlements are actually made at the last minute of the last hour outside the doors to the court. If settlement is not reached within these timeframes, the lender may be held in contempt of the court order, a situation that lenders and their attorneys do not want to put themselves into. Judges are known to come down hard on parties that ignore their orders.

Once the credible mortgage analysis reporting is in hand, the power in these situations stems from understanding the Rules of Evidence. The State Rules of Evidence tend to be more or less similar to the Federal Rules, however, knowing the State's rules is critical.

To get an idea of what the rules of evidence provide for in submissions of evidence, here is an example from the State of Florida.
These rules can be found online in the Florida Statutes ("FS") Evidence Code (Ch 90).
BEGIN CITING:

Matters may be noticed judicially on facts that are not subject to dispute because they are capable of accurate determination by resort to sources whose accuracy cannot be questioned. (FS 90.202(12)).

A court shall take judicial notice when a party requests it and: Gives each adverse party timely written notice of the request with proof filed with the court, to enable the adverse party to prepare to meet the request and respond (FS 90.203(1)), *and furnishes the court with sufficient information to enable it to take judicial notice of the matter* (FS 90.203(2)).

The evidence has to be relevant and tend to prove or disprove a material fact (FS 90.401).

All relevant evidence is admissible, except as provided by law (FS 90.402) *it is not objectionable for the expert to provide an opinion on the ultimate issue if that opinion includes an ultimate issue to be decided by the "Trier" of fact* [the Judge for those unfamiliar with this term - the author] (FS 90.703).

The expert does not have to provide voluminous writings initially to the court, and can summarize, as long as they make the data available for examination or copying or both by other parties at a reasonable time and place.(FS 90.956).
END CITING.

As stated before, if expert testimony is going to be used, the expert will have to qualify on his or her individual merits before the court and may be subject to the adverse parties' scrutiny, so the expert's resume and knowledge must be real and accountable.

Chapter 6

The Battleground is Court by Legal Process

The battlegrounds are in State and Federal courts across America. Each battle is on an individual mortgage for a specific borrower with a uniquely identifiable case. The Congressional legislative intent was to entitle the people and their advocates to fight their foreclosure battle using the Acts, Codes, Regulations, Statutes and Laws. Agencies also fight cases, for example: precedent setting cases where imminent consumer protection is needed, and cases where classes of individuals need protection.

The lender's strategy is simply to win by motion for Summary Judgment. It results in the judge making a determination without a jury or trial, to rule in favor of one side based on the evidence, or lack thereof, submitted into the case or the lack of response from the parties. Summary Judgment is the first wave of the battle in court.

The lender wants to eliminate any possibility of having to go through discovery, answer interrogatories, and provide admissions to allegations by the borrower's attorney or a mortgage analysis expert.

In order to win by Summary Judgment one side will attempt to prove that there are no material facts in opposition to the claims and therefore no issues to be tried. Summary Judgment is the most desirable goal to achieve in court. However, it is a very precarious target for a borrower in a foreclosure case to accomplish. The target for the borrower's attorney is to bring evidence that summary judgment is not appropriate. This is where credible mortgage analysis comes in.

The lender will attempt to persuade the court by making statements and supplying documentary evidence that there are no material facts. NRM Lender attorneys have been known to employ a practice of do anything, say anything, and provide anything to win summary judgment.

Mortgage analysis often finds misrepresentations and flaws in statements, affidavits, documents, and allegations presented when predatory lending is involved. But when a borrower's attorney does not assess mortgage compliance analysis of violations or toxicity and the lender's attorneys are not challenged with evidence to the contrary, or with meaningful pointed discovery and the lender wins in Summary Judgment, for all intents and purposes, the battle is over. The NRM Lender wins foreclosure.

The issue of whether a borrower's attorney can be held financially responsible for not assessing a borrower's position relative to mortgage compliance analysis is a topic of concern. No attorney wants to have a borrower come marching into their offices some time after losing a foreclosure case, with a malpractice attorney in tow, asking to see evidence of an Assessment or other proof that rudimentary research was done in the case, especially when a comprehensive assessment can be obtained in minutes at a nominal charge of less than $100 (at the time of this writing). See www.fpg-usa.com. The malpractice attorney can do the same, and if the results turn violations or toxicity, the problem can become very serious indeed.

Either side can lose to Summary Judgment by not responding to court actions properly or within the time frames allotted as well as failing to persuade the judge that there are significant issues and material facts that prevent a finding of Summary Judgment.

Losing to summary judgment is cold, hard and brutal and in most instances, final. Vacating or overturning the ruling after the fact requires proving misrepresentation and fraud occurred. The reality of that, given the case was tried and these two determinate issues were not raised, or if raised were not proven, makes proving so after the fact a difficult, expensive process with little likelihood of success.

Forensics in that situation is expensive, time consuming and slow. Everything has to be performed manually.

After Summary Judgment, there comes an eviction and sale. Once the foreclosure sale is complete, the benefits of TILA evaporate. One of the criteria for consumer protection under TILA is that the consumer still owns the property.

Battling the foreclosure case to a successful outcome involves a strong borrower's attorney strategy. Lender attorneys have the edge coming into the case. They have a mortgage in default, with rights to foreclosure inherent in the contract. Therefore the burden rests on the borrower's attorney to prove otherwise. The borrower's attorney strategy is simple and straight forward. Speed is of the essence. Perform forensic loan analysis and discovery. Respond promptly by initial procedural response dates with pertinent issues of evidentiary findings introduced into evidence. This shifts the burden of proof to the lender and turns the tide of assumption away from the holder of the mortgage. Promptly perform initial discovery and file "pertinent" first requests for admissions, interrogatories, and documents. "Pertinent" meaning customized to catch the lender red handed if they respond honestly and fully. If the lender fails to respond to the requests, motion for an order from the Judge to perform. If they continue to not perform, move for dismissal with prejudice, meaning the case cannot come back to court. If the case is dismissed without prejudice, the lender can come back to court, starting the process from the beginning, but this time they will have to come with the discovery items clarified because they are going to get hit with that again right off the bat. Anything less may not be considered strategy at all.

A borrower's attorney, who believes simply moving a case sideways without the strategy just mentioned, is kidding themselves. Unfortunately their lack of skill and competence in this arena just prolongs the inevitable foreclosure.

Here are a few reasons why moving the case sideways is a bad idea:

1. A lender faced with a borrower on a refinance loan of a primary residence originated less than three years ago, has the

specter of extended right of rescission, meaning cancelling the loan. This book contains a whole chapter on this important borrower's device of congressionally legislated protection. Suffice it to say, cancelling the loan is very expensive and counterproductive to the NRM Lender. The three year mark is hard and fast. Once it is crossed, the remedy is no longer an option.

2. It often plays into lender's hands because their real estate owned divisions are jammed with properties that are being held back so as not to flood the real estate market all at once, and while the case is moving sideways, the borrower is paying for the upkeep instead of the lender.

3. It will cost the borrower much more in the long run due to accumulating debts, costs, and fees incurred from the lender over time. If and when a settlement is reached, these charges are often tacked on to the mortgage and either amortized over time or paid in a lump sum later in the life of the loan.

4. The lender moving on a dual track of foreclosure and entertaining loan modification is most often holding the "carrot" of modification out to take the borrower attorney's eye to keep them off the real target, foreclosure. An incorrect but naturally assumed philosophy, is that pressing hard legally against foreclosure may create a bad feeling and hamper loan modification settlement. Nothing could be more false. If the lender is not put in an untenable position in court with credible mortgage analysis findings of violations or toxicity, the chance of a good settlement in many cases, is simply lost. Here is why:

Lenders avoid settling and modifying loans despite what is being "said", for a few basic reasons. Unless the borrower's attorney puts the lender over a legal barrel, the lender motivations to foreclosure are simply too strong.

- Legal exposure to the investors. What may be good for one class of investors is likely not good for another. The specter of a class action lawsuit by the tranche slice investors who are hurt as the result of a loan modification that benefits other tranche slice holders in the mortgage pool can result in the Trustee being forced to sue the NRM Lender, enjoining all investors in the tranche slice that are being hurt with the loan modification settlement. This is a real threat to the NRM Lenders.

- Foreclosure yields profits to the lender even though a loan modification may be beneficial to the investors. In many cases the servicing lender has prior agreement from the investors to credit the lender back with losses or expenses in the process of default loan servicing and foreclosure. There may also be offsets to the investor of insurance proceeds they may have received on the defaulted loan. These and other aspects favor the servicing lender in many cases, walking away with the foreclosed property leaving little or nothing left for the investors.

- The physical burden of modifying a loan, in terms of staff and logistics, is daunting. Even under the best conditions it strains the corporation servicing the loan. In today's environment, with bankruptcies and failures of lender participants, the problem is made even worse. Add the complexity of the National Servicing Platforms, the necessity for the Trustee of the investor pool Trust and others involved required to sign off on loan modifications, the task is often a daunting process even for the Lender desiring to modify a loan.

- Bringing the issue of fighting a lost or stolen note claim and finding undisputable evidence that the loan was not properly transferred in accordance with the pooling and servicing agreement in a securitized loan brings additional problems. The lender may be faced with purchasing the loan back from the Trust as a matter of pre-agreement. When one loan is discovered to contain this flaw, the Trustee might cause other loans in the Trust to be evaluated. A lender faced with multiple loan buybacks at full initial mortgage loan amounts, on loans currently in default, can face huge financial losses. The fact that this process could clear ownership issues for the foreclosing lender is no consolation. Lenders who have already been paid in full for selling a mortgage to the investor pool do not want to give that money back and have the privilege of foreclosing. They want the home gifted to them in foreclosure, even though they cannot establish rightful ownership.

Many states do not require court cases and legal actions for lenders to foreclose. In these states, the borrower has pre-agreed in the Deed of Trust, the mortgage document, to foreclosure without legal action.

This is the issue of judicial process vs. non-judicial process.
To complicate matters of deploying legal strategy once mortgage analysis and discovery producing violations and toxicity has been performed, some states have a judicial process and others have a non-judicial process and some states have both.

Judicial process means that the borrower is served legal papers and given time to respond. In the non-judicial process the borrower is at a much greater risk. Understanding the critical aspect of process is paramount. Judicial or Non-Judicial Process? That is the question.

No one wants to get a knock at the door from the Sheriff with an eviction notice. Or, come home to find one posted on the front door. Worse yet, is to come home to find furniture and possessions on the sidewalk. This can happen without the borrower knowing in a non-judicial process where sheriff's service of an initial complaint is not a requirement. Many borrowers have stopped answering phone calls and reading mail as a self preservation technique against collection activities. While this is the wrong approach, it is commonly understood by lenders and government sponsored enterprises such as Fannie Mae who has issued collection guidelines that include a visit to the home, in an effort to protect borrowers from their own habit of avoiding calls and mail.

To make matters worse, some states practice both processes. It is very important to determine exactly what the particular state's process is for a given loan facing foreclosure. Because this is such a critical issue, the following briefly describes the particulars of each process in greater detail.

In a Judicial process state the borrower will be well noticed. The borrower is served with court papers (a lis pendis, summons and complaint) and the case proceeds in court. A pending litigation notice (the lis pendis) is recorded so the public knows there are legal issues facing the property; the borrower is served with a complaint which they must answer in a prescribed time and fashion, and the case will be heard in court. The lender will likely allege there are no material issues to discuss and move for Summary Judgment. If Summary Judgment is awarded, the court will order a sheriff's auction sale where the property goes to the highest bidder and will be sold for cash or a big deposit and balance due in x days (ex: 30). The court will confirm the sale and a sheriff's deed will be issued and subsequently recorded with the county clerk. The highest bidder is now the owner of the property.

In a non-judicial process state the borrower must know the specific procedure under which they will receive notice in their state. There are several methods, none of which is as clear and decisive as in a judicial process state where the borrower is officially served. The notice may not require direct owner notification. It may simply require an ad in a publication. It may be a Notice of Default, a Notice of Sale, etc. Non-Judicial foreclosures are processed without court intervention. Therefore, it is critical that the borrower check their mail and take action when the Default Letter or Notice of Default arrives.

In non-judicial process the borrower may have to bring a lawsuit against the lender if the borrower wants to challenge the foreclosure. Otherwise, the home could simply be foreclosed by the lender properly posting, recording, and/or publishing a notice as required in the appropriate clause of the Deed of Trust or other appropriate mortgage document and then whenever the legal time limit for the borrower's state expires, a public auction is held, the highest bidder wins and becomes the owner subject to recording the deed. Cash or cash equivalent is typically paid at the auction or very soon after. This is the scenario where the Sheriff turns up and puts the borrower and their belongings on the curb or street.

Non-judicial foreclosure process may be used if the mortgage or deed of trust contains a "power of sale" clause that serves as the borrower's pre-authorization to sell the property to cover the debt in the case of the borrower's default. The power is usually given to the lender or their representative, usually called the Trustee.

Always consult the particular documentation and the State's rules. Seek professional counsel. To see how the process of non-judicial foreclosure under the power of sale clause works, here is an example from Nevada.

A copy of the notice of default with the election to sell is delivered to the borrower at their last known address. Notice is recorded in the county in which the property is located and this date is posted. Postings and advertisements are handled in the same manner as execution sales. The borrower has a specified time to respond (fifteen to thirty five days) based upon the original Deed of Trust, to cure with payment. The property owner may file Intent to Cure with the public Trustee's office at least fifteen days before the scheduled foreclosure sale day and pay the amount due prior to the sale date. The foreclosure sale will take place as specified. Lender attempts to claim deficiency judgment for the difference of the sale amount yielding less than the amount due, must be made within three months. Borrowers have no rights to redeem, meaning to recover the property by coming in after the foreclosure or tax sale and paying off the amount owed.

Defendant vs. Plaintiff
In addition to the complications of judicial vs. non-judicial process, many people mistakenly refer to borrowers facing foreclosure as the defendant, or as the plaintiff. It all depends on the process of the state in which the property is located. For example, in Florida, the borrower is usually the defendant in a residential mortgage foreclosure. Florida is a judicial process state. In California or Nevada for example, the borrower would be the Plaintiff under their non-judicial process residential foreclosure action rules.

In a judicial process state the borrower has been sued for foreclosure by the lender. This makes the lender the Plaintiff (the one who is complaining and files a complaint). The borrower is the Defendant (defends against the complaint).

It is the reverse in a non-judicial process. The lender is provided the rights to foreclose in the loan documents and does so according to the prescribed process. When the borrower feels they have evidence or allegations to fight against the foreclosure in court, the borrower must become the Plaintiff and file a lawsuit by complaint against the lender who becomes the defendant.

Mortgage or a Deed of Trust (Trust Deed)?

Deed of Trust

Many people have difficulty in understanding a Deed of Trust. A loan is taken out and the actual title is held by an independent 3rd party (such as a title company) until the deed of trust is paid off in full, at which point they issue a satisfaction and the Original Title. In the event of a default, the Trustee holds the "power of sale" and files a Notice of Default or similar instrument under the judicial process rules required in the particular state that holds jurisdiction. In default, the trustee holding the title will likely bring in and substitute a different trustee (under the substitution clause) specialized in handling foreclosure.

There are 3 parties to the Trust Deed.
1. Beneficiary: The lender.
2. Trustor: The borrower (also called grantor).
3. Trustee: The 3rd party that holds legal title.

Some states call their deed of trust a "mortgage deed of trust" or "mortgage deed" or "security deed". If the word "deed" is used, it is usually a deed of trust situation. Check the particular documentation and seek professional advice.

Mortgage and Note

A mortgage serves as security for a debt. The note is a written promise to pay and includes specifics such as interest rate, payment time, etc. The original "blue ink" signature on that note insures it is the one and only true original. A photocopy is worthless without material stipulations and conditions to the contrary.

The mortgage does not present the type of loan and repayment plan a borrower has. This is defined in the note. For example, the NOTE can be a Fixed Rate (FRM), an Adjustable Rate (ARM), an Interest Only (IO); and the amortization terms of the NOTE define the maturity and whether or not there is a balloon payment, prepayment, negative amortization on the mortgage, etc.

There are 2 parties to the Mortgage and Mortgage NOTE:
1. Mortgagor: Borrower
2. Mortgagee: Lender

Other important items to know in regards to a specific state:

The general "uncontested" time between a Notice of Default and a Foreclosure Sale can vary depending on the State the property is in. For example, as little as two (2) months in Texas, a fast foreclosure state, to New York where the process can take (10) ten months to a few years.

Is there a Right of Redemption Period and if so, what is it? The right of redemption period is the time after the property has been sold at auction, in which the borrower may legally buy back the property from whoever purchased it at auction.

Is there a right to a Deficiency Judgment? This gives the lender the right to chase the borrower for years to come. The deficiency is the total amount of money owed the Lender, minus the amount collected from the sale of the property.

To complicate matters, many states have both Mortgage and Deed of Trust instruments. It will depend upon the actual instrument the borrower has. Investigate the foreclosure procedures and rules in the state in question via reliable legal resources.

In a non-judicial process state, the evidentiary findings produced as a result of credible mortgage analysis are normally sent to the lender's legal department with a legal letter advising of the imminent action if the case is not in court already. If the case is in court, the lender's attorney will be advised in the normal course of civil procedure. This, coupled with a borrower ready, willing, and able to settle on a loan modification, with some money in escrow for that purpose, may aid in negotiating a fast and satisfactory settlement. Otherwise, in the legal process of fighting foreclosure, costs will be borne by both parties including legal fees, court costs, and third party services such as compliance analysis and discovery.

Side Stepping Losing The Rights To Foreclose In Court

It is important to note that servicing lenders sell loans to side step losing the rights to foreclose in court.

What I mean by side step is the following. NRM Predatory lenders are known to use devious tactics to try to side step the courts when cases go against them. A case in point can be found in the Commonwealth Of Massachusetts, Plaintiff Vs. Fremont Investment & Loan, and Fremont General Corporation "Fremont"; dated March 2008, civil action 07-4373-BLS1; *the court was taken by surprise. The court admitted failing to anticipate that Fremont, in the face of a court ordered injunction preventing Fremont from foreclosing on some 2,200 homes without following strict notice to the MA Attorney General; would simply attempt to side step losing in court and transfer servicing rights to an entity that would simply pick up the forecloses as if nothing had happened.*

Eventually, Fremont was found to be predatory and the borrowers were protected by the court, but not without extensive and expensive litigation.

Fremont, being a perfect example of the predatory NRM Lender, was used to manipulating courts at will up until the State of Massachusetts case. Fremont argued that in restricting them like this, no servicing entity would assume the servicing rights. This argument wasn't accepted by the court, who essentially responded that they could sell the servicing but the restrictions on foreclosure proceedings must pass with the sale attached to the individual loans. The court was fooled initially because Fremont alluded to going out of business. The court has since learned the lender's tactics of not divulging truthful information and included the knowledge obtained in the Courts' decision.

Fremont was caught red handed. The court found that they unfairly issued loans that borrowers couldn't afford and because of the terms, were not able to refinance. The court issued an injunction that unless the transfer of servicing included provisions to extend the protection against foreclosures, the court would simply prevent the deal from closing.

Then the Federal Deposit Insurance Company "FDIC" entered the fray. The FDIC found that Fremont was undercapitalized and failed to comply with capital provisions. Fremont had to either sell enough shares of the Bank to adequately capitalize or find and agree to being acquired by another bank.

If the FDIC took over Fremont, the pooling and servicing agreement's defaulted servicer provisions would automatically trigger and by law, the servicing rights would automatically be assigned to a third party that wasn't bound by the court ordered injunction thereby leaving the Massachusetts homeowners open to unrestricted foreclosure.

Fremont made some agreements and the Massachusetts court agreed not to enjoin Fremont from selling the loan servicing to another entity. In total there were some 2,200 loans originally covered in this lawsuit.

Chapter 7

Loan Modification: The Options to Save or Sell

Section I. Options to Save Your Home

1. Forbearance
2. Loan Modification-Restructuring
3. Partial Claim (for FHA and some Freddie Mac Investor Loans only)
4. Refinance
5. Reinstatement
6. Repayment Plan
7. VA Loan Modification/Refunding

Section II: Options to Sell Your Home

1. Assumption
2. Deed-In-Lieu
3. Pre-Foreclosure Sale
4. Sale
5. Short Sale

LOAN MODIFICATIONS: THE OPTIONS TO SAVE OR SELL[2]

If and when a loan modification settlement becomes a real and imminent possibility, it is important to know one's options.

Outside third party professional advice should be sought in every case from the outset, whether that is legal, accounting, real estate, lending or anything else that pertains. It is always important to get more than one opinion.

Borrowers can mix and match some of the alternatives. The object is for a long term solution that works. When a borrower is upside down on the mortgage a lowering of the principal amount of the loan to 80% or 90% of the current market value of the home is a good start. If the lender insists on using their own appraisal then the borrower should acquire three appraisals in total and select the middle appraisal amount to set the new modified loan to value.

The lender may agree to accept some escalating percentage of potential appreciation in market value over a period of some years to come, in exchange for lowering the principal amount of the loan. This is known as a SAM, Shared Appreciation Mortgage. It is also a government sponsored option and should be researched. Borrowers should be aware of other government sponsored options as they come out. The internet is an excellent up to the minute source of loan modification information.

Borrowers should beware of any loan with escalating mortgage interest rates that offer to settle the borrower's problem over a few years but result in the very same problem down the road. There are no guarantees that the real estate markets will reverse and that the appreciation will facilitate a permanent refinance sometime in the future with good terms.

---

[2] The content in the notated section of this chapter was taken with permission from Whale Mortgage, a Florida correspondent lender the author owned and operated for years. Whale Mortgage is no longer in business. Whale Mortgage had no complaints or violations against them on record and never had to buy back a mortgage.

Section I. Options to Save Your Home

If a borrower is currently employed and has sufficient income to make payments and carry his / her home expenses, or if the borrower is currently UN-employed but with a previously good payment record and with good prospects for employment in the near future, the borrower might have the following options:

1. Forbearance
2. Loan Modification-Restructuring
3. Partial Claim (for FHA and some Freddie Mac Investor Loans only)
4. Refinance
5. Reinstatement
6. Repayment Plan
7. VA Loan Modification/Refunding

1. Forbearance

The lender may allow the borrower to reduce or suspend payments for a short period of time and then agree to another option to bring the loan current. A forbearance option is often combined with a reinstatement when the borrower knows they will have enough money to bring the account current at a specific time. The money might come from a hiring bonus, investment, insurance settlement, or tax refund.

2. Loan Modification-Restructuring

(Available on all conventional loans, also on a very limited number of VA loans with lender and/or investor approval) (Called Recast for FHA)

A loan modification to an existing loan made by a lender/servicer in response to a borrower's long-term inability to repay the loan. Loan modifications typically involve a reduction in the interest rate on the loan, an extension of the length of the term of the loan, a different type of loan or any combination of the three. These will result in lower payments. A lender might be open to modifying a loan because the cost of doing so is less than the cost of default.

A loan modification agreement is different from a forbearance agreement. A forbearance agreement provides short-term relief for borrowers who have temporary financial problems, while a loan modification agreement is a long-term solution for borrowers who will never be able to repay an existing loan.

There are costs and fees associated with a modification that the borrower will be responsible for. All property taxes must be current or the borrower must be participating in an approved payment plan with the taxing authority to be eligible for a modification. Any additional liens or mortgagees must agree to be subordinate to the first mortgage. All requests are subject to the lender's approval.

3. Partial Claim (for FHA Loans and some Freddie Mac Investor loans)

A borrower may be eligible for a partial claim. The loan must be 120 to 365 days past due. A partial claim results in placing the past due payments into a subordinate mortgage (2nd mortgage) between the borrower and the Secretary of Housing Urban Development. The partial claim note will require the borrower to start making payments when they pay off the first mortgage. Working together with The Department of Housing and Urban Development (HUD), the lender will agree to help the borrower with a one-time payment from the FHA Insurance Fund. There is no interest. The partial claim can be for no more than 12 months of past due payments. The borrower will be required to sign a promissory note with HUD and they will place a lien on their property. This HUD loan is interest-free and will bring the account up to date immediately, but it is due when the borrower pays off the first loan or when the property is left or sold. The borrower will not be required to make monthly or periodic payments. The note is payable to HUD. Partial payments can be made but they must be by cashier's check or certified funds. There is a lifetime limitation of 12 monthly installments of PITI (Principal, Interest, Taxes and Insurance). The Partial Claim may be combined with another plan. In some cases, a special forbearance may be combined to give the home owner some additional options.

4. Refinance

In some instances, the borrower may be able to arrange new financing, but this will depend on their income, their credit report, the value of the home, the amount of their equity and their current financial position. It will be difficult to secure new financing with a default on the existing mortgage, but not impossible. A poor credit score may be outweighed with the following: Good equity in the property, a good reason why the borrower's credit is bad and solid evidence of how the current financial situation has changed. The last 12 months of credit history will be examined very closely.

5. Reinstatement

This is probably the least likely to occur, except in special circumstances where the borrower now has all the money to catch up completely, in a lump sum, including back payment and attorney fees. To become current, the payment must be made by a specific date. Because of the borrower's financial circumstances in the past, they may be facing a sizable amount of past-due fees, including back payments, late fees and legal expenses. If the borrower is able to promise a lump-sum to bring the payments to a current status by a specific date, the borrower may be eligible for a Reinstatement.

Many borrowers have retirement funds, credit cards or insurance policies that can provide the much-needed funds to stay secure in their home. Other borrowers will seek private loans from family or friends or co-workers.

6. Repayment Plan

If the borrower has incurred a short term financial hardship and the loan is 62 days or more past due, the borrower may be able to get a written agreement to resume making regular payments and agree to add some amount of money (ex: a few hundred dollars) per month to bring the deficiency current or put some of the deficiency onto the back of the loan (or a combination of both), until the loan is caught up. There will be a specific period of time to bring the loan current. A repayment plan is accepted by all investors and is the most frequent method of curing a default. Realistically, a repayment plan does not go any longer than 24 months and with private Wall Street money does not extend past 12 months without approval. The borrower's financial situation must be closely reviewed for this option to be considered. Borrowers must show they can afford this plan, to be eligible

7. VA Loan Modification/Refunding

(Available for VA loans only) (Needs at least 30 days to process) A refunding is when the VA buys the loan from the lender. Refunding may give VA the flexibility to consider options to help the borrower save the home that the current lender either could not or would not consider. When the VA refunds a loan under 38 U.S.C. 36.4318, the delinquency is added to the principal balance and the loan is re-amortized. The new loan will be non-transferable without prior approval from the Secretary. If the borrower's interest rate was lowered and an assumption was approved, the interest rate will be adjusted back to the previous rate.

Section II: Options to Sell Your Home

Short Payoffs (Short Sale), Pre-foreclosure Sale, Compromise of Sale. If the borrower is unable to maintain the property and make the payments, the financial hardship is long term. The property is upside down, meaning the mortgage amount is higher than the market value of the property. Short payoffs avoid a default loss on the property. Lenders may accommodate a short payoff with a qualified buyer at the ready. Contact a tax advisor because there are tax ramifications and time limits associated with short payoffs. Some states allow lenders to seek deficiency judgments for the difference in sale amount and loan amounts that can allow continued collections on the borrower for years to come.

1. Assumption
2. Deed-In-Lieu
3. Pre-Foreclosure Sale
4. Sale
5. Short Sale

1. Assumption

A mortgage assumption permits a new qualified borrower to take over both the title to the property and the mortgage obligation from the current borrower if the borrower is behind in payments. An enforceable "due-on-sale" clause is waived to allow the qualified buyer to assume the mortgage of the delinquent borrower

2. Deed-In-Lieu

As a last resort, the borrower "gives back" the property and the debt is forgiven. This will not save the home, but it is less damaging to the borrower's credit rating. The tax ramifications may be more appealing, especially if the home was purchased as an investment property. This option might sound like the easiest way out, but it has limitations: The borrower will usually have to try to sell the home for its fair market value for at least 90 days before the lender will consider this option. To be considered for this option, the borrower must complete a financial package and provide a copy of a recent active listing agreement. Also, there cannot be any claims or liens (ex: IRS or state tax liens) against the property other than the mortgage. In exchange for the deed-in-lieu, the lender may waiver all deficiency judgment rights. The borrower may be asked to participate in a Short Payoff program before a deed-in-lieu of foreclosure is accepted.

This is a lender's last resort to helping a homeowner avoid foreclosure. The lender takes a property back and manages it until it is disposed, sold, and off the books. Lenders would rather do a short sale as a liquidation technique than Deed-In-Lieu.

When a property has substantial equity, it may make sense for the lender to take a property. Substantial equity might allow a lender to sell the property quickly.

Deed-In-Lieu allows a property owner to surrender the property back to the lender/investor/servicer and to be released of the mortgage obligations. This is only a last ditch effort and is taken only if it makes sense and the lender feels they can market the property faster.

Qualifications are that the property has been listed for sale and no reasonable offers even less than the BPO (Broker's Price Opinion) have been made. There must be a cost savings rather than going to an auction/sheriff sale

3. Pre-Foreclosure Sale
If the borrower can't sell the property for the full amount of the loan, the lender may accept less than the amount owed. Financial help may also be available to pay other lien holders and/or help towards some moving costs. The borrower may qualify if: The loan is at least 2 months delinquent; the borrower (or their real estate professional) can sell the house within 3 to 5 months; a new appraisal (obtained by the lender) shows that the value of the home meets the lender's program guidelines.

4. Sale
If the borrower can no longer afford the home, the lender will usually give the borrower a specific amount of time to find a purchaser and pay off the total amount owed. The borrower will be expected to use the services of a real estate professional who can aggressively market the property.

5. Short Sale
A short sale is the sale of a property at fair market value, when the lender and or insurer agree to accept the proceeds of the sale in satisfaction of the defaulted mortgage even though it is less than the amount owed.

Generally a short sale should be considered when the homeowner's financial hardships require that they sell their home, but faces problems selling because the value of the property has declined to less than the amount owed on their mortgage.

A short sale may be considered at any time prior to foreclosure if the alternative means a lender will incur greater losses through foreclosure and be forced to acquire the property.

In order to consider a short sale, a homeowner or real estate professional must submit a signed purchase contract and a HUD 1 settlement statement.

Once the purchase and sales agreement and the other documents needed are submitted the qualification process begins.

Pre-Qualification Process

The pre-qualification program can run 90 to 120 days prior to the actual short sale date. This time is used to list the property at fair market value to obtain a purchase and sale agreement. If a contract is received the loan will be submitted for a short sale.

There are numerous processes to handle during this phase. These include qualifying the borrower, qualifying the property, negotiating and obtaining a satisfactory approval letter, marking the property to market, working with realtors, buyers, etc.,

Short Sale Negotiations

The short sale negotiations begin once an offer is received. A signed contract is received by a potential buyer offering a price and sometimes with contingencies.

There are numerous processes to be handled during this phase. They include documentation required, analysis, validation, settlement terms, confirmation of intent, qualifying the buyer, negotiation and mediation with the lender, examination of lender documentation, conformity with the guidelines, putting foreclosure on hold and performing all the necessary functions to facilitate the closing.

One important point to remember about modifications if the borrower is facing foreclosure is THE COLLECTION ACTIVITY WILL CONTINUE WHILE NEGOTIATIONS ARE UNDER WAY. Do not fall into the lender's trap by not preparing to legally face foreclosure while negotiating any type of settlement. Many foreclosure disaster stories stem from making this mistake only to find out the home was lost in foreclosure by Summary Judgment.

Chapter 8

Special Tax Considerations for Investors

There are significant tax ramifications in the forgiveness of debt for investors. These are real concerns that need to be planned for and understood in advance of agreeing to a particular settlement. Speak to an accountant beforehand. Borrowers get a surprise when the bank sends them a 1099 of some sort with 'phantom income' reporting (income where no cash or tangible asset was received). The appropriate relief should be included in any settlement agreed to. Once it's over, it's over and the borrower does not want to be answering to Uncle Sam if not prepared.

Investors need to take special care in their workouts because what may seem like a reasonable settlement, even if it means signing a note to the lender, can backfire immensely when the IRS tax implications are factored in.

Some investors are clamoring to do short sales, meaning the lender agrees to accept less than the outstanding loan balance as a settlement to sell the property to a new buyer. The bank gets the bad debt off their books. The owner is out of the loan, or so it seems.

At the time of this writing, IRS Publication 544 is the pivotal document for determining the tax due on the amount "forgiven" in this type of transaction. Owners who live in the property do not get taxed on amounts forgiven because of recent changes in the tax law. The same protection is NOT available for investors. It is very difficult to trick the IRS (unlike many lenders) into believing the loan was for an "owner occupied" property if, in actuality, it wasn't. At the time of this writing, the test for owner occupancy is in IRS Publication 982.

The investor has two worries. 1) The lender releasing the Owner from ever coming back at them for a deficiency judgment if the lender realizes less in the sale then the mortgage amount and 2) IRS taxes.

A 1099A (for foreclosure) or a 1099C (for short sale) is going to be issued to the Owner and IRS taxes will apply to an investor. The basis of computing the amount owed is clear. The amount realized includes the FULL CANCELED DEBT, even if the fair market value of the property is less than the canceled debt.

Example: John paid for or built a house costing $400,000. He put $30,000 down and borrowed the remaining $370,000 from a bank. The bank foreclosed or a short sale was done. The balance of the loan was $360,000 and the property sold for $260,000. The amount realized by John on the sale is $100,000 for tax purposes, which is the debt canceled by the foreclosure or short sale. This is calculated by comparing the amount realized ($360,000) with the adjusted basis ($260,000).

The above example poses 2 issues:

1: Without written notice or laws in the state where the property was located stating otherwise, the bank can come after John for the $100,000 difference. This is called a deficiency judgment, and

2: John will receive a 1099-C from the bank for $100,000 which they will also report to the IRS. John will add $100,000 to his ordinary income for the present tax year and have to pay income taxes on this at John's tax rate.

In a best case scenario above, John is going to pay a great deal more in taxes. If John is in the 30% tax bracket, he will be faced with paying an additional $30,000 ($100,000 X 30%) to the IRS.

Owners who fail to consider the potential future collection rights BEFORE they decide on settlement, especially the tax ramifications, may just be jumping from the frying pan into the fire.

John's problems may be compounded if he built his home at a time when the market was rising and his construction loan allowed him to borrow a percentage of the finished home's appraisal value. Here's why: Take the above example with this one twist: John built it for $400,000 but when it was finished it was worth $650,000 and he took a permanent loan using his same deposit of $30,000, for $620,000. Now John realizes $620,000 owed minus the $260,000 sale or a gain of $360,000 and in the 30% tax bracket $120,000 is owed the IRS.

It is important to consider all aspects of the borrower's situation prior to making decisions. The object is to rid the borrower of headaches. The borrower should seek professional advice, whether it is legal, accounting, real estate, lending, or other.

PART TWO

Diagrams of a
Securitized Transaction
With Key Notes

Useful For Building a Foundation
Based on Evidence in Court

Diagram of a Securitized Subprime Transaction

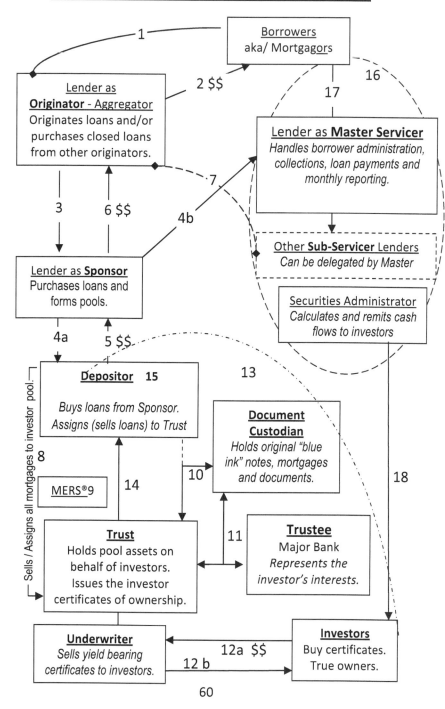

Part Two

Diagrams and Information

Mastering the use of the diagrams in the following chapters is critical to winning against foreclosure.

With the exception of the first diagram, all essentially employ the same basic structure. However each diagram has a different section highlighted which represents the aspect covered in that particular section.

Securitization of the type covered in this book and illustrated in the following pages is one of the most complex corporate banking transactional enterprises in the history of modern banking and securities. If it was not, media, government, politicians, lawyers, judges and borrowers would already know the enterprise and this book would not be necessary. The purpose of the following chapters is to make it easy and understandable to everyone, not just the financial elite.

As Musashi Miyamoto, Japan's greatest swordsman of the 16th and 17th centuries wrote in his memorable book of warfare entitled The Book of Five Rings "learn this well, make it yours". It is said that his last guides before dying were the way of walking alone and the way of self reliance.

This is what it takes nowadays to win against foreclosure. The diagrams and their text are important to winning. In a similar way to the great swordsmen wielding two swords, a long and a short sword, the warrior against foreclosure wields two swords, Lender Compliance Analysis [SM] and Forensic Lender Discovery [SM] (both covered in Part Three). To facilitate wielding them well, you must understand the target. This is the purpose of the diagrams section here in Part Two of this book.

Diagram of a Securitized Subprime Transaction

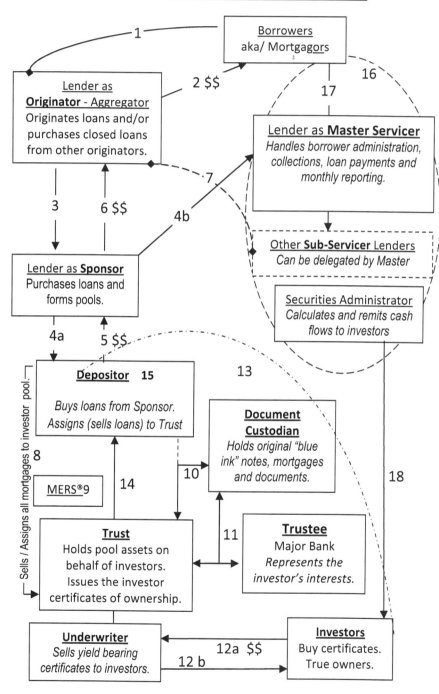

Chapter 9

Diagram of a Securitized Subprime Transaction

The numbers beside the following key notes are synchronized with the corresponding numbers on the diagram referenced. This first diagram in the series is built on a basic diagram that would typically be printed in a Prospectus of the proposed transaction. Identifying numbers and the money flow have been added for better understanding.

1. Borrower applies for loan. Gives original "blue ink" signed copy of Mortgage and Note to lender.

2. Lender funds loan to borrower by monies received from the mortgage pool investor contributions or by an interim short term loan to be repaid by mortgage pool investor funds.

3. Lender gathers loans it has originated and or purchased and gets ready to switch hats and become Sponsoring lender. Any loans bought have to be properly transferred and noted in property records. This is a requirement of subsequent sale by the Lender when wearing hat of Sponsoring lender, formally selling the loans to the Depositor.

4. a) Lender wearing hat as Sponsor sells loans to Depositor who can only accept legally transferred loans properly recorded with Depositor as legal rightful owner according to the Pooling and Servicing Agreement and laws of the individual States, modeled after the Uniform Laws. Lender no longer has any legal right or claim to ownership of mortgage.

b) Reserves rights to *servicing* each borrower's loan in the pool but retains NO OWERSHIP RIGHTS.

5. Depositor pays lender wearing hat as Sponsor in full for the entire face value of the loan amount *plus* a Servicing Release Premium (SRP). SRPs arc not required to be divulged on the borrower's Hud-1 settlement statement. Instead a mortgage servicing disclosure is required, the failure of which to include in a loan document package to the borrower can result in a TILA[3] and a RESPA[4] violation.

6. Sponsoring lender repays any lenders on loans it purchased from others.

7. Participating lenders may receive sub-servicing privileges arranged by Sponsoring lender or otherwise given by Master Servicer.

8. Depositor sells or otherwise transfers all loans to the pool of investors represented by the Trust.

9. The Loan Originator may have designated MERS® status as an electronic system to track the servicing lenders on the loan. Where assignments of the mortgage are necessary to facilitate servicing, MERS® status can be updated electronically. The Document Custodian keeps the blue ink signed copy of the original mortgage with endorsements, transfers and assignments noted either on the face of the note or on a permanently attached paper for the purpose, called an allonge. Loan servicing transfers do not include the original mortgage note. While loan servicing changes hands regularly as a practical matter, the original mortgage note stays with the Document Custodian who safeguards the originals from ever being lost or misplaced.

---

[3] Truth in Lending Act
[4] Real Estate Settlement Procedures Act

MERS® never has anything whatsoever to do with the original Note at any time, either by possession or reference. It never sees or knows of the original note.

MERS® provides voluntary appointment of a representative at the servicing lender to facilitate subsequent transfers of servicing rights. For example, an administrative assistant at the lender may be endowed with the title of V.P. of MERS®, in order to facilitate loan servicing transfers. However it should be noted that this individual receives no compensation from MERS®, is not an employee of MERS® and is under no ethical obligation or direction of the MERS ® Corporation. Rather they are an employee under control and direction of the servicing lender.

MERS® is merely an electronic database entity that anyone can sign up for if they pay the nominal fee. It was created by the mortgage banking industry to facilitate transfers of servicing rights. Every MERS® loan is issued an eighteen digit MIN number and anyone with a computer connected to the internet can log into the MERS® web site to see who the current servicer is on any MERS® loan. This information can also be supplied with address and/or borrower's name. The search is not wholly reliant on the MINS number. The MERS® web site also provides contact info on the current servicer. This is useful for loans in transfer. It is important to be in contact with the current servicer and not the servicer who has recently sold the servicing rights to another servicer.

10. Depositor causes the one original "blue ink" signed mortgage and note to be properly recorded in the appropriate state county clerk's office of the state in which the property is physically located, then makes a true sale of the mortgage and note with proper assignment to the Trust, and delivers the underlying original mortgage note to the Document Custodian as per the Pooling and Servicing Agreement, on behalf and at the instruction of the Trustee, representing the investors who have purchased the individual loans for inclusion into the pool. The Trust is the current holder of the transferred note. The Trustee

often delegates the checking of individual mortgage notes to the Document Custodian for a fee. The Document Custodian thereby confirms the appropriate assignments on the face (usually on the bottom) or on a stapled attachment called an "allonge" which becomes a permanent part of the note itself. The last endorsement is drawn to the specifically named Trust of the same name that the investor's certificates of trust ownership bear.

11. The Trustee of the Trust relies on the Master Document Custodian to examine and confirm the original properly endorsed and transferred "blue ink" signed mortgage notes. A top accounting firm will typically come in and confirm or attest, that all the original "blue ink" signed mortgages and notes on each and every mortgage have been properly transferred and recorded in the appropriate county clerks' office of the state in which the property is located. These "valuable originals" are given into the possession of the Document Custodian, typically an entity of extraordinary integrity and experience in safeguarding millions of original documents in folders, stored in boxes in storage vaults. Each one properly checked and filed.

12. a) Investment proceeds paid to Underwriter. The investors put up the pool investment, in cash. In the case of this example, this is one billion dollars ($1,000,000,000.00) in cash. The money is released upon confirmation of receipt of the "blue ink" signed originals and the accounting firm's attestation that indeed all mortgages paid for are properly accounted for in original form, with proper transfers and stored in safe keeping with the Document Custodian. The funds which have been held by the Underwriter, a major investment banking firm, are released.

b) Underwriter issues certificates to the Investors. These certificates represent ownership of the underlying mortgages in the pool.

13. The transactions inside this arch are specifically notable by what is missing, not what is shown. Subsequent diagrams will include all. It is interesting to note that the Prospectus which claims to divulge all may do so in writing but not in a diagram like this one. Notably missing are the hidden profit center operations that will be revealed in subsequent diagrams. This includes the Special Purpose Vehicle, CDO Manger, pooling of the mortgage notes, upgrading the credit and inclusion of the notes in derivatives called Collateralized Debt Obligations. The tranche slices and the residual shareholders that receive mortgages which bear credit ratings that are just too poor to sell into the pool.

14. Underwriter deducts their fee and hands over the balance of funds received by the investors to the Trustee on behalf of the Trust. The Trustee deducts their appropriate fees and pays the appropriate parties. This includes paying the Depositor in full for the all the mortgages the Trust purchased in the pooled transaction.

15. The Depositor is a legal entity whose purpose is to buy the mortgages destined for a designated Trust, ensure the proper recording, and sell the mortgages in the transaction to the Trust. Once completed, the Depositor is for all intents and purposes out of the picture. Depositors are often entities created by other entities who have billions of dollars of mortgage accumulation and sale histories, however, the Depositor is established as entity with no track record itself and no assets other than the transient mortgages in the subject pool.

16. The Servicing Loop. Servicing handles collection and interaction with the borrowers and calculation and remission of cash flows to investors. The Master Servicer can delegate sub servicers to deal with borrowers. That typically includes borrower administration and day to day operations, collections, billing, loan payments, escrows, monthly reporting, default servicing, and foreclosure actions. These services are considered to be within the national servicing platforms' influence. This includes legal and accounting.

17. Borrowers make their monthly payments to the designated servicer. This will likely be an authorized sub servicer who has strict servicing guidelines by which to operate. Anything outside the box, for instance a "good long term" loan modification settlement, may have to be presented to the Master Servicer who may require settlement approval by the Trustee. Loan modification settlements often require involvement of the Default Servicing Platform and may require National Servicing Platform participation.

18. The Securities Administrator within the servicing loop calculates and remits monthly cash flows to the investors based on the class of certificates and cap (yield) contractual agreements.

Some real world examples of Lenders who wear the hats of Originators, Sponsors, and Master Servicers at the time of this writing might include EMC Mortgage Company, Litton Loan Servicing, Chase, GMAC, Homecomings, Countrywide, Americas Servicing Company, Aurora Loan Servicing, etc.

Some real world examples of major Trust and Trustee banks at the time of this writing might include JP Morgan Chase, Wells Fargo, Bank of America, Deutsch Bank, HSBC, Countrywide, etc.

Chapter 10

The NRM Lender's Initial Plan: Hide the Profit

At this point, an example using real numbers is useful for examining the profits in just one mortgage pool. For those interested in "running the numbers", the following is broken down into six parts.

1. $400 million: Selling 9% cash flow for 6%.
2. $250 million: Up-tranching (upgrading) borrower credit.
3. $600 million: Re-selling the same mortgages via CDOs.
4. $100 million: Foreclosure with proceeds going to the bank.
5. $50 million: Up-selling.

- $1.4 billion Total <u>Net</u> Profit to the NRM Lender,

  Plus:
6. $800 million investors paid up front to buy the mortgages, essentially resulting in the NRM Lender basically brokering the mortgages into the pools and not lending. The NRM Lenders have NO risk yet much better than merely brokering, the NRM Lender wins the right to steer the servicing contracts.

- $2.2 billion Total <u>Gross</u> Profit to the NRM Lender

The profits above represent just one of the thousands of pools sold over the six or seven year beginning in the year 2000, following the repeal of the Banking Act of 1933 less than 60 days earlier, in November of 1999. It was these trillions in *fabricated* profits that caused the Meltdown of 2008 disaster which affected world economies. Many brilliant minds "in the know" warned, but apparently no one really listened. Warnings memorialized in speeches, testimony, interviews, letters, and newsfeeds.

The following breaks the profits down into the parts using dollar amounts. Examples are based on a pool of mortgages with eight hundred million dollars ($800,000,000) in total originated mortgage amount. The profits compute up easily to two billion two hundred million dollars ($2,200,000,000) in six general parts.

Part 1: *Selling cash flow at a premium.* To profit from selling cash flow at a premium, the NRM Lender simply sells loans they acquire at a higher percentage, to investors at a lower percentage. This is a four step process.

1. NRM Lender goes out and buys, or originates 4,000 loans for $200,000 each on average. That is $800 million. NRM Lender can do this many times per month, considering the investor demand out there. So this first transaction is going to be a template for an assembly line of similar transactions.

2. The subprime borrowers that make up each pool have an average mortgage payment of 9% across all loans in the pool. This includes an 8% average for first position loans and for those that are using a first and second loan, a 12% average on the second loan. All totaled the average mortgage payment interest rate borrowers across the pool are paying is 9%. Nine percent of $800 million in loan amount is a yearly income of $72 million. This 9% income is funded by mortgage payments from the borrowers. The true credit score on borrowers paying 9% average on their mortgages is below 620.

3. A Wall Street Underwriter is brought into the transaction. The Underwriter commits to bring investors in to buy the entire pool of mortgages. These investors are willing to accept a 6% return on average credit borrowers, which is a better return in the market place that what is available from average credit company long term debt in the form of bonds. Corporate bonds are also taxable while the pool has tax pass through benefits that further enhance the pool's cash flow attractiveness to investors.

4. The first business profit model the NRM Lenders will perform is transforming $72 million (9% annual mortgage income) based on $800 million in mortgages into $1.2 billion.

This yields three immediate benefits.
   a) An immediate $400 million profit, and
   b) The purchase of $800 million and all the loans, so the NRM Lender is essentially acting as a broker without one dime of risk in the underlying loans. Buying the mortgages transfers the risk of default to the investors who purchase them.

The transaction is simple. Divide the $72 million dollar ($72,000,000) cash flow being paid by the borrowers on the entire group of mortgages going into the pool, by 6%, the cash flow that these mortgage pool investors are willing to accept. The investors pay $1.2 billion ($1,200,000,000) in exchange for receiving a cash flow averaging 6%. This brings nice neat net profit of four hundred million dollars ($400,000,000) to the NRM Lender within a very short time, sometimes days, of the mortgages being pooled. This is Part 1 of the Income Projections for the NRM Lender.

Sub-Total Part 1: *Selling cash flow at a premium.*
Profit: $400,000,000 ($400 million) paid at closing.

Part 2: *Up-tranching (upgrading) borrower credit.* A bond market technique of breaking the different underlying credit of individual borrowers in mortgage pools into groups called tranches (means "slices" in French) that are sold to investors of pooled mortgages. Up-tranching involves upgrading the borrower's credit via Swap derivatives that serve to entice credit ratings agencies to raise the credit based upon insurance representations against default of the mortgages. This is traditionally done by the CDO Manager in the hidden profit area of a securitized transaction and is detailed in the upcoming diagram in Chapter 11 entitled The Lenders Hidden Profit Centers.

Assuming that only one quarter of the four thousand mortgages had their credit upgraded, this equals one thousand mortgages. Assume an average face value of each mortgage at $250,000 and the amount comes out to about $250 million ($250,000,000) of mortgages in this upgrading of credit scenario. These numbers are actually very low as this is a conservative example (Discovery will uncover the real numbers). If the true mortgage monthly payments from borrowers are at an average interest rate of 8% per year, this is a total cash flow of $20 million ($20,000,000) per year. Assume the ratings agencies place an "AAA" value on the resultant tranche grouping, taking into consideration the credit default swap insurance placed on the tranche grouping. Then, assume that on "AAA" rated bonds with tax pass through preferences, as is the case in the mortgage pools, the investors are willing to accept 4% cash flow. This amount is significantly higher than they can receive in the bond markets or from banks. Simply dividing the 4% into the available $20 million of available cash flow to distribute, this provides a $250 million ($250,000,000) profit paid to the NRM Lenders at or shortly after the loan closings and sale of all the loans in the pool to investors.

Sub-Total Part 2: *Up-tranching (upgrading) borrower credit.*
Profit: $250,000,000 ($250 million). Paid shortly after closing.

Part 3: *Reselling the same mortgages via CDOs.*
Repackaging mortgages in synthesized collateralized debt obligations and credit default swaps takes place in the Depositor, Special Purpose Vehicle and CDO Manager phase of a securitized transaction. The diagram section of Chapter 11 entitled The Lender's Hidden Profit Areas details the process. Simply put, the selling and reselling of the original note is a matter of offering investment derivative bonds made up of cross collateralization of the same mortgage over and over again. While statistics show there were many trillions of these sub-prime class investment vehicles out on the market prior to the Meltdown of 2008, reliable sources claim there were only about $1.2 trillion of the mortgages themselves.

Many banks and investment houses were holding what they thought were trillions upon trillions of dollars worth of CDO assets. For example, Bear Stearns alone, the first big investment house to collapse, was holding some 12 trillion in CDOs. The total of CDO assets held by the biggest players in the marketplace just prior to the collapse, represented many trillions of dollars. The Federal Reserve Board, the Securities and Exchange Commission, and the Federal Accounting Standards Board understood this.

This knowledge spurred these entities to institute the Mark to Market requirements which many blame for triggering the Meltdown Of 2008. Under Mark to Market, the holders of CDOs were forced to estimate their holdings based on the current value of the assets instead of the perceived value over the length of the instrument, for example thirty years on an underlying thirty year bond or mortgage. Within one financial quarter, this simple action decimated these holdings. This caused capital ratio violations, which caused rampant selling of everything that could be turned into cash, including stocks and other liquid assets, which caused margin calls which caused more selling. Reselling mortgages en masse, blended into CDOs, is surprisingly easy. A marketplace was created to facilitate this and the transactions were conducted like any other bond transaction, albeit the product was not the traditional bond most were used to.

There is no way to tell exactly how many times a particular mortgage was sold and resold into CDO form on a particular transaction unless discovery is conducted. NRM Lenders and the parties involved are naturally resistant to divulging the information for obvious reasons. Many of the supposed high credit bonds, as history confirms, are now valued as junk bonds valued at pennies on the original price paid by investors.

For the purposes of this example, only one half of the total upgraded credit mortgages were resold ($600 million of the $1.2 billion sold). This number is more likely a gross understatement as reselling loans multiple times was quite common.

Sub-Total Part 3: *Reselling the same mortgages via CDOs.*
Profit: $600,000,000 ($600 million) paid shortly after closing.

Part 4: *Foreclosure with proceeds going to the bank.*

With millions of mortgages in foreclosure and over fifteen thousand occurring per day (according to recent news reports), it is difficult to discern the exact number of mortgages foreclosing in a particular pool. In the marketplace this book covers, the NRM Lenders subprime markets, the percentages are very high.

In this example, there are $800 million in original face amount of mortgages represented by 4,000 individual loans. Some assumptions must be made to produce a number to tag to this part of the NRM Lender profit equation.

Assume a 50% default rate. In other words, four hundred million in underlying mortgages where borrowers cannot pay their payments for one reason or other. In most cases the mortgage payments have recast or the interest adjusted to a higher rate. For whatever reason, the defaults are a staggering historical event at this point.

Continuing with these assumptions, the fifty percent defaulting represent 2,000 mortgages. Assuming these properties are foreclosed upon and in the process, the servicing lender has claims to amounts collected before payments are made to the investors, the calculation of distribution of foreclosure sale proceeds must include deductions for insurance proceeds received by investors on the defaulted loans. It must also take into account amounts spent by the servicing lender in the foreclosure process. Rather than take a higher number, in keeping with assuming the most conservative side of the possibilities, assume that only fifty thousand $50,000) dollars from each property is net realized gain to the NRM Lenders from each foreclosure. That number is likely far higher. At the fifty thousand number per foreclosed home, two thousand homes sold at "fire sale" prices will yield a net profit to the NRM Lenders of $100 million dollars.

Sub-Total Part 4: *Foreclosure with proceeds going to the bank.*
Profit: $100,000,000 ($100 million) at foreclosure.

Part 5: *Up-selling foreclosed properties for a profit.*
Again this number is hard to come by without proper discovery. Homes that are taken by NRM Lenders in foreclosure are often purchased by the NRM Lender at the fire sale prices under the guise of

clearing up title. Title issues on foreclosed homes present a problem, especially when the original note is not produced. Title issues are an impediment to selling foreclosed homes that have not been purchased first by NRM Lenders but are purchased directly from the foreclosed homeowner. Assume, for argument's sake that on the 2,000 foreclosed homes won in foreclosure, reselling only produces $25,000 each in profit to the NRM Lender. This token amount should allow the homes to still sell below market price and ensure a fast turnaround. 2,000 homes times $25,000 each is $50 million dollars ($50,000,000).

Sub-Total Part 5: *Up-selling foreclosed properties for a profit.*
Profit: $50,000,000 ($50 million). At sale of foreclosed property.

In summary of the profit part projections add the following:
1. $400 million: Selling cash flow at a premium..
2. $250 million: Up-tranching (upgrading) borrower credit.
3. $600 million: Re-selling the same mortgages via CDOs.
4. $100 million: Foreclosure with proceeds going to the bank.
5. $50 million: Up-selling the foreclosed properties.

- **$1.4 billion Total <u>Net</u> Profit to the NRM Lender**, not including:

6. $800 million investors paid up front to buy the mortgages, essentially resulting in the NRM Lender basically brokering the mortgages into the pools and not lending. The NRM Lenders have NO risk yet much better than merely brokering, the NRM Lender wins the right to steer the servicing contracts, sell the cash flow at premiums, upgrade the borrower credit, resell the same mortgages via CDO's, benefit from insurance premiums paid by investors in Swaps, gain profits by foreclosing and then selling the foreclosed properties at below market values afterwards. This combination produces a substantial two billion two hundred thousand dollar ($2,200,000,000) profit for the NRM Lender acting as a glorified mortgage broker. What is more, this is only on ONE transaction. The NRM Lenders were churning transactions out like an assembly line prior to the Meltdown of 2008.

- **$2.2 billion Total <u>Gross</u> Profit to the NRM Lender**

This was a very conservative example, unfortunately for borrowers and investors the actual NRM Lender profits are often MUCH higher, In any event the actual profits are able to be quantified as the result of Discovery. Discovery of this information is vital to protecting the borrower's interests as well as the investors'. Forensic Lender Discovery ^{SM} is the tool that is used to empower an attorney on a borrower's behalf, to begin to uncover this information. When used properly, in accordance with the rules of evidence, this method of discovery is an awesome weapon against the NRM Lender in court. This subject will be discussed in more detail throughout this book.

Chapter 11

Secrets Behind Lender Operations in 13 Diagrams

In the previous chapter, an example of the hidden profit areas NRM Lenders utilize in their operational structure was laid out. The numbers placed in the profit zones are "guestimates" gleaned from experience the field. The hidden operations are important to understand if one aspires to bring the profits to bear in court or settlement. NRM Lenders are crying wolf in court and before Congressional committees and the media. In this way the foreclosures are being given to them in most cases, without proper credit for the hidden profits the NRM Lender's earned using the predatory mortgages as product sold and resold for tremendous profits. The devil, as the saying goes, is in the details.

Forensic Lender Discovery [SM] is the tool used to ascertain the actual numbers of the different areas and operations discussed in the last chapter. This provides a way to arrive at a profit scenario. A Judge may then be motioned (asked in a legal sense) to notice and evaluate the findings. If a Judge determines that the profit earned by the NRM Lender entitles the borrower to offsets as a defensive recoupment or counter claim, the borrower can benefit in a meaningful way. The lender faced with this scenario may well in advance of discovering the total financial aspect of hidden profits, allow the case to be negotiated for a long term loan modification settlement or a sale in which the borrower simply walks away and is not chased for years to come.

In this way, NRM Lenders screaming about losses, when they actually earned extraordinary profits, can be confronted with those profits in court. Especially an NRM Lender refusing to perform a legitimate long term loan modification that works for a borrower.

These diagrams are presented in the following pages:

- The Lender's Organizational Structure
- What Lenders Want the Borrower To See
- The Lenders Hidden Profit Centers
- Document Custodian Holds the Original "Blue Ink" Signed Note
- The NRM Lender's Bankruptcy Protection Layer
- Two Separate Recorded Sales From Originator to Investor
- Special Purpose Vehicle (SPV) Smoke and Mirrors
  - Collateralized Debt Obligations
  - Credit Default Swaps
  - Equity of mortgages with credt too low to resell
- Collateralized Debt Obligations Manager
- MERS® Exposed, Tool for Ownership Deception
- Lender Objectives in Court – 3 Diagrams
  - What Lenders Want the Court to Believe
  - What Lenders Do NOT Want the Court to See
- The Hidden National Servicing Platform Layer
  - National Servicing Platform,
  - Information Service Provider,
  - Default Solutions Provider,
  - Foreclosure Mills,
  - Default Servicing
  - Dual Tracks to Foreclosure

The Lender's Organizational Structure

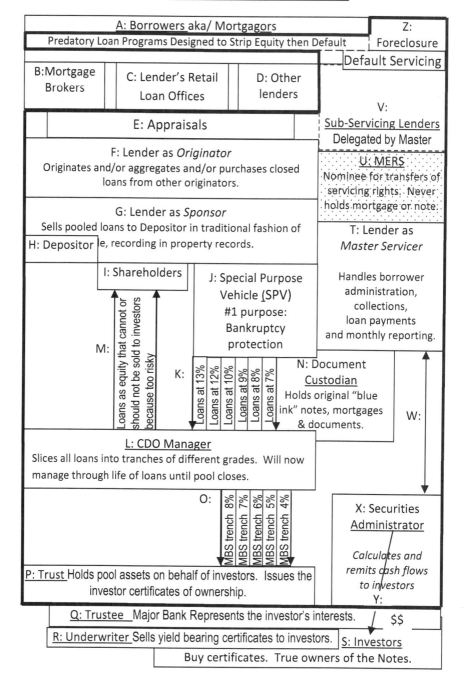

A: Borrowers aka/ Mortgagors

Z: Foreclosure

Predatory Loan Programs Designed to Strip Equity then Default

Default Servicing

B: Mortgage Brokers

C: Lender's Retail Loan Offices

D: Other lenders

V: Sub-Servicing Lenders Delegated by Master

E: Appraisals

F: Lender as *Originator*
Originates and/or aggregates and/or purchases closed loans from other originators.

U: MERS
Nominee for transfers of servicing rights. Never holds mortgage or note.

G: Lender as *Sponsor*
Sells pooled loans to Depositor in traditional fashion of [sal]e, recording in property records.

H: Depositor

T: Lender as *Master Servicer*

I: Shareholders

J: Special Purpose Vehicle (SPV)
#1 purpose:
Bankruptcy protection

Handles borrower administration, collections, loan payments and monthly reporting.

M: Loans as equity that cannot or should not be sold to investors because too risky

K: Loans at 13% | Loans at 12% | Loans at 10% | Loans at 9% | Loans at 8% | Loans at 7%

N: Document Custodian
Holds original "blue ink" notes, mortgages & documents.

W:

L: CDO Manager
Slices all loans into tranches of different grades. Will now manage through life of loans until pool closes.

O: MBS trench 8% | MBS trench 7% | MBS trench 6% | MBS trench 5% | MBS trench 4%

X: Securities Administrator
Calculates and remits cash flows to investors
Y:

P: Trust Holds pool assets on behalf of investors. Issues the investor certificates of ownership.

Q: Trustee Major Bank Represents the investor's interests.

$$

R: Underwriter Sells yield bearing certificates to investors.

S: Investors
Buy certificates. True owners of the Notes.

- **The Lenders Organizational Structure**

The Investor side of these transactions is governed by Securities and Exchange Commission (SEC) rules requiring full disclosure. The dominant document that controls all aspects of the mortgage backed securities transaction is called the Pooling and Servicing Agreement. The Prospectus, given to prospective investors, also bears importance. Promises and procedural descriptions in these documents must be followed or criminal charges and other remedies may be pursued by government agencies charged with that responsibility. These and others documents filed over the course of the transaction are considered sworn federal SEC filings.

Examples of formal documentation used in the transactions are:
1. The Pooling and Servicing Agreement: In general, the parties include the Depositor(H), the Trustee(Q), the Master Servicer(T) and, in some cases, a Special Servicer(V), and a Securities Administrator(X).
2. The Prospectus and Supplements: Wherein all parties to the pooling and servicing agreement will be identified.
3. The Master and Sub-Servicer Servicing Agreements
4. Credit Enhancement Agreements
5. Interest Rate Cap and Cash Flow Agreements
6. Owner Trust Agreements – The Bond Indentures
7. Legal and Accounting Reporting Agreements
8. Swap Agreements and Swap Counterparty Agreements
9. Lender Mortgage Repurchase Agreements
10. Depositor Shareholder Agreement (private)

What Lenders Want the Borrower to See

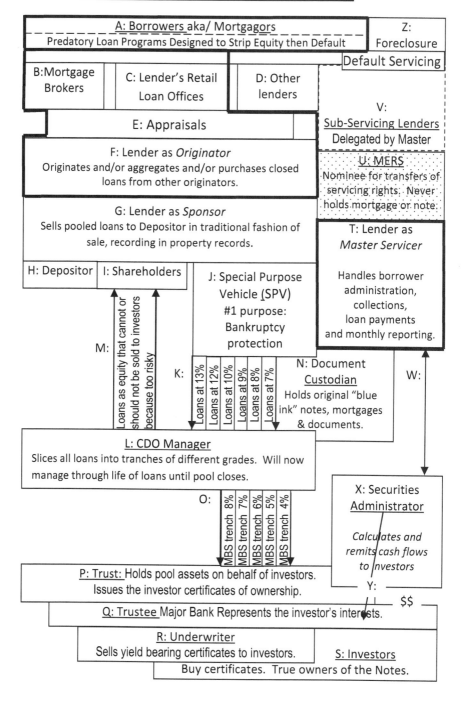

- **What Lenders Want the Borrower To See**

Lenders want the Borrowers(A) to see them as traditional lenders, not profiteers in desperate need to originate loans as a product they will bundle and sell (over and over) in order to fill the tremendous investor demand to buy these loans immediately before or just after closing of the loan to the borrower (A).

If borrowers knew lenders were buying and then selling their loans to investors like hot cakes to earn double, triple and more of the loan amount in profits as well as being paid off for the loan right away, the borrowers might rightly demand better terms and perhaps profit sharing.

Traditionally in banking, this type of profiteering on an asset owned by the borrower, requiring a borrowers cooperation, could be considered a joint venture and as such properly allocate some measure of profits to the borrower in the transaction. Equity, the process of fairness would seem to dictate this.

In the case of the NRM Lender, not only is this equity not offered, the NRM Lender is intent on hiding their profits and taking the borrower's equity on their most important asset, their home, and foreclosing without a measure of remorse. In the process of deceit, NRM Lenders go out of their way to portray themselves as lenders in the traditional sense of making and servicing loans, which they are definitely not. However, to this end the NRM Lenders like to represent aspects of their operations that share similarities to traditional lenders.

1. Good strong Mortgage Broker relationships (B).
2. Active Lender loan offices (C).
3. Responsible Appraisal (E) services.
4. The lender as Originator (F). Lenders do not want the borrower to see their loan is a product to be sold by a lender for tremendous profits. They want to simply be seen as originators.
5. The lender as the servicer on the loan (T). Not a lender whose intention is to sell and resell the loan servicing to others for additional profit over the course of the loan.

In short, NRM Lenders have no qualms about misleading the borrower or the court, or anyone else who will listen.

The Lenders Hidden Profit Centers

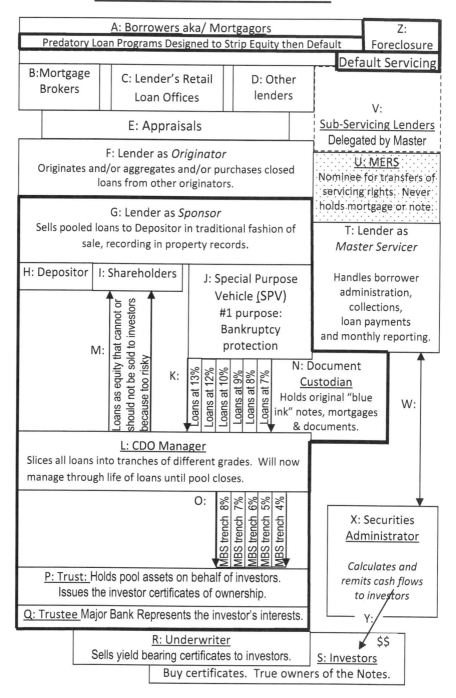

A: Borrowers aka/ Mortgagors
Predatory Loan Programs Designed to Strip Equity then Default

Z: Foreclosure
Default Servicing

B: Mortgage Brokers

C: Lender's Retail Loan Offices

D: Other lenders

E: Appraisals

V: Sub-Servicing Lenders Delegated by Master

F: Lender as *Originator*
Originates and/or aggregates and/or purchases closed loans from other originators.

U: MERS
Nominee for transfers of servicing rights. Never holds mortgage or note.

G: Lender as *Sponsor*
Sells pooled loans to Depositor in traditional fashion of sale, recording in property records.

T: Lender as *Master Servicer*
Handles borrower administration, collections, loan payments and monthly reporting.

H: Depositor

I: Shareholders

J: Special Purpose Vehicle (SPV)
#1 purpose: Bankruptcy protection

M: Loans as equity that cannot or should not be sold to investors because too risky

K: Loans at 13% Loans at 12% Loans at 10% Loans at 9% Loans at 8% Loans at 7%

N: Document Custodian
Holds original "blue ink" notes, mortgages & documents.

W:

L: CDO Manager
Slices all loans into tranches of different grades. Will now manage through life of loans until pool closes.

O: MBS trench 8% MBS trench 7% MBS trench 6% MBS trench 5% MBS trench 4%

X: Securities Administrator
Calculates and remits cash flows to investors

P: Trust: Holds pool assets on behalf of investors. Issues the investor certificates of ownership.

Q: Trustee Major Bank Represents the investor's interests.

Y:

R: Underwriter
Sells yield bearing certificates to investors.

S: Investors
Buy certificates. True owners of the Notes.

$$

- **Uncovering The NRM Lender's Hidden Profit Centers**

CDOs and Swap Deriviaties may be one of the most misunderstood investment vehicles, yet they were and remain some of the most heavily traded investment securities on the market today. Demystifying them will uncover additional aspects of the 2008 Meltdown. These hidden profits are pertinent to winning against foreclosure directly and understanding them will shed light on what triggered the Meltdown of 2008.

At Least Two True Mortgage and Note Sales Must Take Place.

One important ancillary aspect to the hidden profit area is not in actual finances but rather, in establishing, for the record, the true sale of the mortgage note.

The pooling and servicing agreement, the pivotal federally filed (SEC) document outlining the investor's pooled mortgage trust investment, confirms at least two true sales of the mortgage note take place in the securitized transaction.

The one, from the Depositor (H) to the investor Trust (P) is most important and material to who currently owns and holds the properly transferred note.

The toxic flaw that Forensic Lender Discovery [SM] often evidences is that the lender attempting to foreclose does not own and hold the properly transferred note, even though they may misrepresent ownership and falsely claim lost or stolen note status in court to win the home in foreclosure when they do <u>not</u> have legal rights to do so.

Unfortunately, little deterrence exists in courts when lenders attempting to foreclose are caught misrepresenting true ownership to win foreclosure in court.

One of the results of the winning against foreclosure process is proving the party attempting to foreclose has not provided evidence in court that they have the standing, the right of ownership, and thereby preventing a foreclosure from taking place.

There are three basic profit vehicles in the hidden profits area.
1. The Collateralized Debt Obligations (CDOs)
2. The Credit Default Swaps (Swaps)
3. Fees and shareholder ownership of mortgages sold into the pool but not included in either of the above.

The CDOs are the groups of mortgages, called "tranches" sold to investors.

The Swaps are a form of insurance the Issuer (NRM Lender) organizes for substantial fees from the investors that serve to enhance the credit of the groups of mortgages in the CDOs.

These activities take place under the auspices of several participants to the securitized transaction.

A Depositor (H) corporation entity will be formed for the special purpose and existence of buying the mortgages from Lender as Sponsor (G). The Depositor (H) will be an entity that initially has no tangible assets or value.

The Depositor (H) will give shares of ownership back to the Lender as Sponsor (G) as well as other participants in the securitization under shareholder agreements. The Depositor (H) will establish some sub corporations or affiliated entities, including the Special Purpose Vehicle (J) ("SPV") and CDO Manager (L) to perform the actual CDO and Swap creation and development into products that will be sold.

The Depositor (H) is typically a shell corporation established for the sole purpose of accumulating the mortgages and then reselling them through the hidden profit area. The CDOs and Swap transactions will first be sold to investors in the pool, and then sold to cooperating counterparties and then into the open market. The Depositor facilitates the lender side profit operations before selling the mortgages into the pool.

The Depositor may issue shares in itself or an affiliated enterprise created in between the Special Purpose Vehicle (J) and itself. These shares represent NRM Lender ownership through the Originator (F) and Sponsor (G). Shares may also be issued to participants in the securitization such as the Trustee (Q), CDO Manager (L) and Master Servicer (T).

The Special Purpose Vehicle (J) (SPV) is a bankruptcy protected entity with no employees, created to effect the repackaging of the mortgage assets into the CDOs and Swaps. This entity is created for the purpose of facilitating transactions, creating a capital structure that will be sold to investors in the pool, sold to other parties in the securitization and then sold into the open market.

An individual or corporate entity known as the CDO Manager (L) will be brought into the mix to effect the CDO and Swap transactions that will run through the SPV, employing various strategies.

Hidden Bank Profit Operations
The hidden profit operations are within the darkened highlighted areas and take place in H-I-J-K-L-M-N-O. On top of the tremendous profit potential selling "air as gold", there was never one shred of risk to the NRM Lenders in the mortgages themselves. Investors paid the NRM Lenders in cash, in full, with profits from cash flow markups, up front, at closing for the mortgages placed into the pool. So again, the NRM Lenders never had one cent of risk. It was profit from day one.

The whole point of Forensic Lender Discovery ^{SM} is to make this clear to a Judge. If the information is not provided by the parties seeking to foreclose in response to discovery requests made by the borrower's attorney, judges interested in learning the true figures and participants may respond to a motion request and order production. If the lender still refuses or delays and ignores a judge's order(s) settlement in the form of concessions to the borrower including a good long term loan modification become a real option. Judges do not take kindly to having their orders ignored or to misrepresentation and fraud to win foreclose using deceitful practices.

Document Custodian Holds the Original "Blue Ink" Signed Note

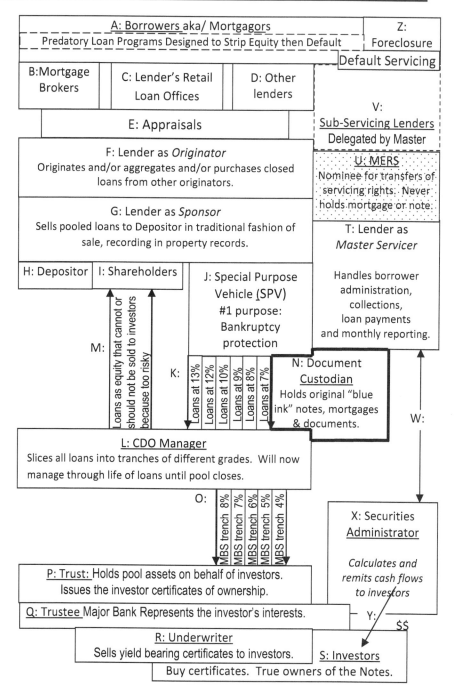

A: Borrowers aka/ Mortgagors
Predatory Loan Programs Designed to Strip Equity then Default

Z: Foreclosure
Default Servicing

B:Mortgage Brokers

C: Lender's Retail Loan Offices

D: Other lenders

V: Sub-Servicing Lenders Delegated by Master

E: Appraisals

F: Lender as *Originator*
Originates and/or aggregates and/or purchases closed loans from other originators.

U: MERS
Nominee for transfers of servicing rights. Never holds mortgage or note.

G: Lender as *Sponsor*
Sells pooled loans to Depositor in traditional fashion of sale, recording in property records.

T: Lender as *Master Servicer*

Handles borrower administration, collections, loan payments and monthly reporting.

H: Depositor

I: Shareholders

J: Special Purpose Vehicle (SPV)
#1 purpose: Bankruptcy protection

M: Loans as equity that cannot or should not be sold to investors because too risky

K: Loans at 13% | Loans at 12% | Loans at 10% | Loans at 9% | Loans at 8% | Loans at 7%

N: Document Custodian
Holds original "blue ink" notes, mortgages & documents.

W:

L: CDO Manager
Slices all loans into tranches of different grades. Will now manage through life of loans until pool closes.

O: MBS trench 8% | MBS trench 7% | MBS trench 6% | MBS trench 5% | MBS trench 4%

X: Securities Administrator

Calculates and remits cash flows to investors

P: Trust: Holds pool assets on behalf of investors. Issues the investor certificates of ownership.

Q: Trustee Major Bank Represents the investor's interests.

Y:
$$

R: Underwriter
Sells yield bearing certificates to investors.

S: Investors
Buy certificates. True owners of the Notes.

- **Document Custodian Holds the Original "Blue Ink" Signed Note**

NRM Lenders would have the courts believe that they are in possession of the original note. This may be true if they are the Originating lender, but the note has subsequently undergone at least one true sale and most likely two true sales in the process of being transferred to the Trust (P) on behalf of the Investors (S) who paid in full for the mortgages that were securitized in the pool.

The Pooling and Servicing Agreement (PSA), the Federal S.E.C. filed document that controls the securitization will be very clear at least on the true sale from the Depositor (H) to the Trust (P). In the sale process a Document Custodian (N) takes responsibility for the actual physical original note properly endorsed to the Trust (P).

NRM Lenders often make a "lost, stolen or destroyed note" claim and sign the affidavit themselves. Or the Servicer signs the affidavit. Or, as in many cases, the NRM Lender supplies the old original note, the one given by the borrower before the loan was sold into securitization, and misrepresents that original note by claiming it is the original, but not the current properly endorsed original which is what the court is looking for to evidence proper current ownership since the note has been sold since it was originated. This current properly endorsed original was placed into the possession of the Document Custodian (N) by order of the Trustee (Q) on behalf of the Trust (P) of Investors (S), shortly after the mortgages in the pool were sold to the investors.

NRM Lenders often allege in court that the note was lost or stolen but that claim does not come from the entity in possession of the originals from the time of note sale to the investors; the Document Custodian (N).

There are important reasons the NRM Lender is willing to get caught in a misrepresentation or fraud charge by the Court, rather than request the original blue ink signed copy of the note from the Document Custodian (N). The issue is the Document Custodian. Too many know too little about this very important entity who according to the PSAs and Prospectus and numerous other agreements, is the entity presented with the properly transferred current original documents including the note.

Fannie Mae, Ginnie Mae and Freddie Mac, put out very detailed information about Document Custodians, their qualifications, responsibilities, The Comptroller of the Currency Administrator of National Banks puts out a 107 page handbook on the topic. Freddie Mac's Document Custodian handbook[5] is 92 pages. The Ginnie Mae Document Custodian Manual[6] is 251 pages. Detailed Document Custodian functions are contained within the over 1225 pages of the Fannie Mae Selling Guide.

In short, Document Custodians are highly qualified regulated entities. This is because of the importance and value of the original notes. It is pertinent to know, that in all cases, the Document Custodian may keep electronic documentation and transmit this. Ledgers, statements and electronic records are accepted. Documents are accepted in scanned digital form. ALL EXCEPT THE ORIGINAL NOTES AND THEIR RECORDING DOCUMENTS. Those must be kept and safeguarded to highly detailed specifications by entities who meet these difficult qualifications.

NRM Lenders detail the selection of a Document Custodian in the PSA. Document Custodians are sometimes referred to as Master Document Custodians, which signifies their ability to delegate other document custodians who meet the requirements of a document custodian, to handle the documents in a particular pool of mortgages. Sometimes a document custodian is merely referred to as Custodian in some pooling agreements.

Whatever the name, document custodians are custodial institutions that meet eligibility criteria. Sellers themselves or servicers and affiliates of the seller may act as document custodians for mortgage loans if they meet the criteria of the custodial institution. Sellers may also negotiate custodial arrangements with an eligible third party document

---

[5] Some information in this section has been paraphrased from the Freddie Mac 92 page Document Custody Procedures Handbook

[6] Some information in this section has been paraphrased from the 251 page Ginne Mae Document Custodian Manual 5500.3 Rev 1.

custodian. When using a government sponsored enterprise like Fannie Mae or Freddie Mac or Ginnie Mae, sellers can use these agencies as their document custodian in accordance with their document delivery systems.

The relationship of the Document Custodian to the Trust of Investors, as typically stipulated in the PSA, is a matter of written agreements with detailed responsibilities noted.

Basically, the document custodian is charged with reviewing and examining each mortgage loan received from the seller (Depositor (H)) to the buyer (Trust (P) on behalf of Investors (S)). The document custodian ensures that all the required documents are received and that they conform to all the provisions of the Document Custodian Agreement (or name of similar meaning).

Document Custodians are often National Banks under the auspices of the Federal Deposit Insurance Corporation (FDIC) and a reference to the FDIC having access, including supervisory agents and examiners of the FDIC is normally included.

Document Custodians that provide custody services to Trusts and Investors with property in the United States, as are the mortgage pools discussed in this book, endeavor to be approved by Fannie Mae, Ginnie Mae, Freddie Mac, and the FDIC and as a Private Investor Custodian. This provides a wide variety of options including agency and private label certification on any type of collateral. In addition to the mortgages held, there are hidden lender profit area transactions that may require a document custodian, such as the collateralized debt obligations and credit default swap derivatives discussed earlier.

The following detail some of the responsibilities and the role a document custodian assumes in the typical mortgage pool transaction.

A contractual master custodial agreement (specific forms for different agencies) will set forth the responsibilities of the issuer and the document custodian. This formally establishes the relationship for safekeeping the loan documents contained in the pool.

Safekeeping requirements will detail the physical protection responsibility and precautions to protect the documents from fire, theft, misplacement or other circumstance. This will include storage safekeeping obligations in secure fire-resistant facilities that prevent unauthorized access to documents and maintain control over all the documents received. It will also include insurance coverage in the event of loss, a material issue to be raised in a lost or stolen note claim by an NRM Lender in a foreclosure action.

Certification requirements ensure the document custodian formally certify each loan in the pool, providing assurance that the documents are complete, consistent and in compliance. This includes the property transfer aspect, meaning proper endorsements on notes and proper recording, review of title and identification of any defects with reporting to the issuer. The document custodian is also responsible for verifying that all the necessary corrections have been made by the issuer before certifying any loan or pool. When a document custodian certifies a pool, they are acknowledging receipt of all documents and that they meet the standards set forth in the PSA. If an agency is involved it also certifies meeting the Agency standards.

Certification is a critical process, as the PSA and Custodian Agreements typically set forth clearly. The reason being that failure to comply with the standards set forth jeopardizes the marketability of the documents. Document custodians, usually banks and Trustees of companies with substantial assets and experience, have very deep pockets (can be sued and held accountable) with significant insurance coverage as well. The document custodian found in violation, such as one who loses or misplaces documentation, deceptively certifies a loan, incorrectly certifies a loan that has not been transferred properly, attests to proper transfer documentation when in fact the note was not transferred properly, or found in any other violations, has significant legal and financial exposure.

In addition to the obvious flaws mentioned in the paragraph above, initial certifications bear a time limitation for final certification. The reason being that initial certifications must occur before the securities are issued to the Investors. A time limit is allowed thereafter to correct any and all defects, but they must all be completed and certified by the

Custodian prior to a specific date. This date will be specified in the PSA and ranges anywhere, for example, from two months out to about twelve months. Consult the pooling documents for the exact date.

It is the Issuer's job to correct the defects, not the document custodian's job. This underlines the significant fear NRM Lenders have in contacting document custodians on foreclosure cases where the NRM Lender in their haste to have the document custodian certify the pool, have misrepresented the proper transfer and recording of notes in accordance with the uniform property transfer rules. The document custodial agreement and the PSA will typically designate a penalty to an issuer for failure to comply with correcting or properly reporting any defects in underlying mortgages. It is simply that the issuer will immediately buy those mortgages back for the price the mortgage was sold to the trust and collateralized in tranche debt purchased by the investors. This protective mechanism is in place to protect the document custodians from deceit and misrepresentation by an issuer, as well as to protect the investors in the pool. Issuers in this case are the NRM Lenders as Originator (F), Sponsor (G) or Depositor (H).

Document custodians are charged with keeping all the pool related documents including the properly transferred original notes in one permanent storage location and identifying this location in the PSA and custodial agreements. Accessibility is required to permit representatives of the issuer (the NRM Lender) Agency representatives, the Trustee of the investor pool or their designees and the Securities Administrator or their designees to have access to and inspect any documents held by the document custodian that relate the specific investor pool.

Document custodian organizations seek regulatory approval as a policy to enhance their reach of services across a wide swath of mortgage pool originations. One of several different agencies may have primary regulatory authority over a document custodian who must be in good standing unless it has had problems and is operating under an approved management plan. Good standing means not being under management oversight of its primary regulator for being insolvent, in receivership, in the process of liquidation or other problematic state. The regulatory agencies include (alphabetically):

- Federal Deposit Insurance Corporation (FDIC)
- Federal Home Loan Bank (FHLB)
- Federal Reserve (FRB)
- National Credit Union Administration (NCUA)
- Office of the Comptroller of the Currency (OCC)
- Office of Thrift Supervision (OTS)

It is appropriate to discuss security measures document custodians have in place to meet agency requirements, because while NRM Lenders have no qualms over routinely claiming lost, stolen or destroyed note status across broad swathes of their foreclosure cases, this is rarely the case. Here's why:

- Document custodians are required to maintain storage facilities with a level of access and security controls that are nothing short of favorably impressive to the mind and senses of any onlooker. For example:
- Documents are usually stored in vaults
- Fire resistant storage (1.5 to 2 hours)
- Secure access controls such as personnel security card readers
- Electronic access records
- Multiple employee presence whenever entering a vault
- Written access logs
- Employment of knowledgeable personnel
- Minimum financial requirements in the form of audited financial statements of the document custodian
- Minimum insurance coverage maintained to indemnify losses including, trust operations errors and omissions, premises insurance, in transit insurance, forgery or alteration insurance fidelity bond insurance. All insurances must be underwritten by a rated financial institution, such as Best's or Lloyds of London for example.
- Established written procedures periodically updated and reviewed.

- Written disaster recovery plans that include facilities restoration, backup and recovery of electronic data and physical recovery of the files.
- A Quality Control Program in place, with recent audits and disclosures made available for inspection and a regulatory disclosure policy to report findings of problems and issues.

Any entity seeking to perform self custodial functions or designate custody by an affiliate or third party will be required to meet the eligibility standards above if any loans are sold to or through Fannie Mae, Ginnie Mae, Freddie Mac. In any event, the document custodian documents and agreements will set forth the standards that must be met. If they allude to any regulatory agency mentioned in the bullet points a few paragraphs above, then the document custodian is regulated and all of the above plus additional controls may apply. This is just a short list; the full responsibilities are stated in hundreds of pages of regulatory guides, manuals and handbooks.

The point is, an NRM Lender frivolously stating a lost, stolen or destroyed note in court is literally making a mockery of the courts' lack of understanding into the functions of a document custodian. This allegation is a serious one to document custodians and the regulatory compliance agencies who require detailed reporting of such instances.

Why then do NRM Lenders risk this obvious misrepresentation bordering on fraud to a court? The answer may be found in the risk reward analysis. The lender caught red-handed in the lie simply receives a verbal admonishment from the court, or perhaps a dismissal with the right to bring the foreclosure action back again. There are no meaningful deterrents to these lies. The reward may be considered stealing the home away from the rightful owner who does have the original note stored with the document custodian, based upon a request to re-issue the note to the NRM Lender or Servicer without any attempt to contact the current owner of the note.

NRM Lenders faced with forced buybacks of defaulted mortgages face a ripple effect when deficiencies of the mortgage are brought to the attention of the Trustee or Document Custodian. It may cause the Trustee to investigate other mortgages for the same deficiencies.

The NRM Lender's Bankruptcy Protection Layer

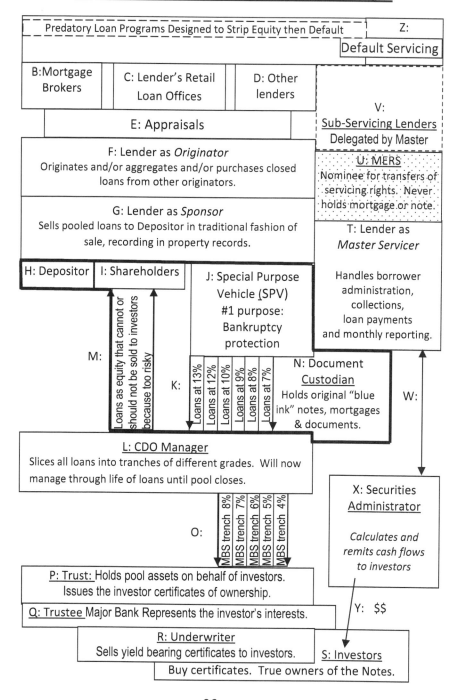

Predatory Loan Programs Designed to Strip Equity then Default

Z:

Default Servicing

B:Mortgage Brokers

C: Lender's Retail Loan Offices

D: Other lenders

E: Appraisals

F: Lender as *Originator*
Originates and/or aggregates and/or purchases closed loans from other originators.

G: Lender as *Sponsor*
Sells pooled loans to Depositor in traditional fashion of sale, recording in property records.

H: Depositor

I: Shareholders

J: Special Purpose Vehicle (SPV)
#1 purpose: Bankruptcy protection

M: Loans as equity that cannot or should not be sold to investors because too risky

K: Loans at 13% Loans at 12% Loans at 10% Loans at 9% Loans at 8% Loans at 7%

N: Document Custodian
Holds original "blue ink" notes, mortgages & documents.

L: CDO Manager
Slices all loans into tranches of different grades. Will now manage through life of loans until pool closes.

O: MBS trench 8% MBS trench 7% MBS trench 6% MBS trench 5% MBS trench 4%

P: Trust: Holds pool assets on behalf of investors. Issues the investor certificates of ownership.

Q: Trustee Major Bank Represents the investor's interests.

R: Underwriter
Sells yield bearing certificates to investors.

V:
Sub-Servicing Lenders Delegated by Master

U: MERS
Nominee for transfers of servicing rights. Never holds mortgage or note.

T: Lender as *Master Servicer*

Handles borrower administration, collections, loan payments and monthly reporting.

W:

X: Securities Administrator

Calculates and remits cash flows to investors

Y: $$

S: Investors
Buy certificates. True owners of the Notes.

- **The NRM Lender's Bankruptcy Protection Layer**

Bankruptcy protection is the number one stated goal in this area of the securitization process. The object is to protect the Lender as Originator (F) and Lender as Sponsor (G) as well as affiliated entities and directors, from a Bankruptcy Court ordering transfers of their Estates to creditors under Section 541 of the U.S. Bankruptcy Code. This insulation layer also protects against claims from lawsuits. Investors are led to believe the bankruptcy layer protects them, which may be true. However, the layer is really there to protect the lenders.

This bankruptcy protection layer may be traversed with critical financial repercussions for lenders. This weakness lies in the issuer (the NRM Lender) requirement to perfect the sale and transfer of mortgages per the Pooling and Servicing Agreement (PSA) or

1) face buying the mortgages back at full face value even if the mortgage is in default facing foreclosure

2) face standing and jurisdictional issues in court because they have sold the notes and mortgages and as such, are not the current owners with rights to foreclose.

NRM Lenders faced with disclosing heretofore undisclosed profits earned on borrower mortgages sold and resold in collateralized debt obligations and credit default swaps may also be financially vulnerable in this area as well.

Claims by lenders that the Depositor (H) and Special Purpose Vehicle (J) (SPV) and CDO Manager (L) are only transitional shell entities that afford bankruptcy protection may be self serving claims designed to deter pursuit. In reality, the Shareholders (S) may facilitate piercing the veil. The CDO Manager manages the mortgage pool for as long as it exists. A case in point is Enron, where the corporations were protected but subsequent actions found executives behind the operations to be held financially accountable. Also, the weakness mentioned in the previous paragraph, buying back mortgages in default, can cripple an NRM Lender.

Two Separate Recorded Sales From Originator to Investor

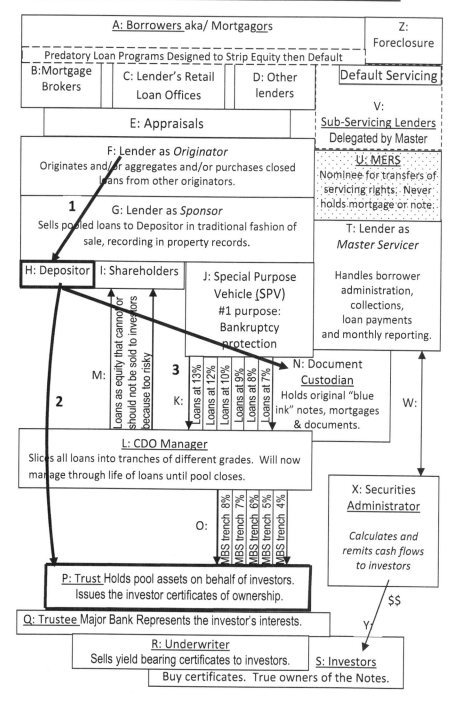

A: Borrowers aka/ Mortgagors	Z: Foreclosure

Predatory Loan Programs Designed to Strip Equity then Default

B: Mortgage Brokers	C: Lender's Retail Loan Offices	D: Other lenders	Default Servicing

E: Appraisals

V: Sub-Servicing Lenders Delegated by Master

F: Lender as *Originator*
Originates and/or aggregates and/or purchases closed loans from other originators.

U: MERS
Nominee for transfers of servicing rights. Never holds mortgage or note.

1

G: Lender as *Sponsor*
Sells pooled loans to Depositor in traditional fashion of sale, recording in property records.

T: Lender as *Master Servicer*

Handles borrower administration, collections, loan payments and monthly reporting.

H: Depositor	I: Shareholders	J: Special Purpose Vehicle (SPV) #1 purpose: Bankruptcy protection

M: Loans as equity that cannot/or should not be sold to investors because too risky

3

K: Loans at 13% | Loans at 12% | Loans at 10% | Loans at 9% | Loans at 8% | Loans at 7%

N: Document Custodian
Holds original "blue ink" notes, mortgages & documents.

2

W:

L: CDO Manager
Slices all loans into tranches of different grades. Will now manage through life of loans until pool closes.

O: MBS trench 8% | MBS trench 7% | MBS trench 6% | MBS trench 5% | MBS trench 4%

X: Securities Administrator

Calculates and remits cash flows to investors

P: Trust Holds pool assets on behalf of investors. Issues the investor certificates of ownership.

$$

Q: Trustee Major Bank Represents the investor's interests.

Y:

R: Underwriter
Sells yield bearing certificates to investors.

S: Investors
Buy certificates. True owners of the Notes.

- **Two Separate Recorded Sales From Originator to Investor**
  Look for at least two completely separate sales taking place in the securitized transaction.
  1. Lender Originator (F) to Depositor (H)
  2. Depositor (H) to Trust (P)

The Depositor (H) makes a true sale to the Trust (P) on behalf of the Investors (S) called certificate holders. The Depositor (H) transfers all rights, title and interest in and to the mortgage loans as identified on the Mortgage Loan Schedule in accordance with the Mortgage Loan Purchase Agreement including, without limitation the right to enforce the obligations of the other parties to the agreement, the right to any Net Swap Payment and any Swap Termination Payment made by the Swap Provider and all other assets included or to be included in the Trust.

The true sale affects three areas concerning borrowers
1. Standing to foreclose – evidence of ownership
2. Proper transfer of the original note precludes lost or stolen note claims
3. Forcing the NRM Lender to repurchase improperly transferred mortgages at their full face value from the Trust of investors. Buying back a mortgage in default can represent a huge loss.

The first two items are straight forward. One must evidence current proper ownership prior to being recognized at law to affect foreclosure. In court, this is called "standing". It is not enough in the process to deliver the original note, since sales have taken place. The original note actually refers to the current properly transferred original note in possession of the current owner.
The third item, repurchased a defaulted loan, is recourse on a loan where the first two items mentioned above have not been properly performed by the issuer.

When and if it is discovered that the original mortgage note has not been properly transferred and recorded according to the terms of the Pooling and Servicing Agreement, and the process to correct the problem has not been solved and effected within the stated period (usually 60 to 180 days), the remedy is simple. The mortgage has to be purchased back at its original face value. This is a strong Foreclosure (Z) stage defense issue.

Buying a defaulted mortgage back at face value will lock the NRM Lender into substantial losses, especially when it is automatic and may alert the Trustee and investors to many mortgages in the same condition and possibly result in a cascade of buy back claims by the Trust of investors, represented by the Trustee. Forensic Loan Discovery [SM] can also be used in this way by the Trustee and Investors as well as by borrowers.
The issue of buying back the defaulted mortgage comes up when the party seeking to foreclose is making lost, destroyed or stolen note claims in a foreclosure case and the paper and affidavit trail are not established to the Master Document Custodian whose charge it is to have and hold the properly transferred original note.

In many cases the NRM Lender does not want to alert the Master Document Custodian or Trustee to the issue so they do not make the proper requests for the original mortgage note. The NRM Lender prefers to risk a court "slapping them on the wrist with a warning or harsh words" than having the Trustee learn of the infraction and order a buy back, as well as a cursory forensic mortgage analysis investigation to assess the extent of this possibility among all the mortgages.

The NRM Lenders may stand on the premise that the Depositor (H) sale to the Trust (P) was completely arms length, and that the Depositor (H) essentially was formed for the purpose of facilitating the transaction and subsequently has little or no substantial asset base. In fact, consulting the typical Pooling and Servicing Agreement it will be noted that it is the Originator (F) or Sponsor (G) who is charged with the responsibility of transferring the loans under the terms of the Agreement. When this is the case, the NRM Lender is caught red handed. A fact that can bring an NRM Lender seeking to foreclose promptly to the negotiating table with a good long term loan modification settlement to a borrower seeking to save or sell their property in a settlement outside of actual foreclosure.

The Depositor:

According to the federally filed documentation known as the Pooling and Servicing Agreement, the Depositor (H) has purchased all the mortgages in the pool and is selling them to the Trust. The Depositor (H) will deliver the original notes with proper transfers noted on them to the Document Custodian (N), at the direction of the Trustee (Q), to hold these most valuable original instruments in safe keeping on behalf of the Trust (P) and Investors (S) in the Trust (P).

Furthermore, in most pooling and servicing agreements, the Depositor sells without recourse for the benefit of the certificate holders all rights, title, and interest of the depositor. The depositor also delivers to the trustee an executed copy of the mortgage loan purchase agreement (or its equivalent titled document). This is a critical discovery document.

The Depositor is relegated by most pooling and servicing agreements to deliver or cause to be delivered, a Prepayment Charge Schedule to the Master Servicer and Trustee on the closing date. This is an integral part of the credit default swaps that will take place and discussed at length in the next diagram, the Special Purpose Vehicle (SPV) Smoke and Mirrors.

In terms of the process creating collateralized debt obligations in tranches that will be sold to Investors, it is also pertinent to know that the Depositor, under most pooling and servicing agreements, may be involved in assessing the credit risk of the underlying mortgages, with notice given by the Depositor to the Trustee and the Master Servicer.

The Depositor has all the pertinent individual loan information. The Depositor's rights and obligations are stated in the Mortgage Loan Purchase Agreement, including the security interest created by that agreement in the mortgages.

Reading a pooling and servicing agreement will bring to light that the Depositor is deeply involved with every party to the securitized transaction, from Originator throughout the different entities involved in the diagram of a securitized transaction, all the way to the final Investors represented as a Trust.

The Depositor is the aggregator of the details as well as the original buyer and seller of the original loan notes and documentation in the securitized transaction. It is the Depositor who sells to the Trust and delivers all the documentation to the Document Custodian and as applicable, to the Master Servicer. In the securitized transaction, these documents are known as the mortgage loan documents and include trailing documents and disclosures required to be included in the mortgage file, at the same time the originals or certified copies are delivered to the Trustee or Document Custodian. The documents include the mortgage policy of title insurance and any mortgage loan documents returned from the recording office.

- Special Purpose Vehicle (SPV) Smoke and Mirrors
  - Foreclosure Discovery
  - Collateralized Debt Obligations (CDOs)
  - Credit Default Swaps (Swaps)
  - Equity of mortgages with credt too low to resell
  - CDOs, Swaps And The Meltdown Of 2008

The Special Purpose Vehicle (J) (SPV) is an entity created under specific Internal Revenue Tax code provisions that provide a source of bankruptcy protection for the Originator (F), Sponsor (G) and other parties who form it and maintain control over it as Shareholders (I). The SPV (J) has no purpose other than the transaction it was created for and no real asset value.

The SPV does its business and then essentially vanishes. There are no employees, no offices, and no real assets. The SPV is a pass through enterprise.

These important NRM Lender profit processes occur in the SPV
- Tranching of the mortgages into Collateralized Debt Obligation groups sold to the investors.
- Credit enhancement of the mortgages in the pool using Credit Default Swaps.
- Stripping highest risk mortgages out of the pool that will be held as investments by the issuer Shareholders (I).

The SPV facilitates credit enhancement and then forms its own capital structure as the tranches of securities are created that will be sold to the Trust (P).The two processes, Collateralized Debt Obligations and Credit Default Swaps are interrelated.

The first to occur is credit enhancement which involves the Credit Default Swaps. Once the credit is enhanced, the Collateralized Debt Obligations can then be sold to the investors. Both of these investment securities, once created, can also trade on the open market where they are sold and resold for enormous profits. First, Swaps are performed to enhance the credit and then the CDOs are sold to investors.

Special Purpose Vehicle (SPV) Smoke and Mirrors

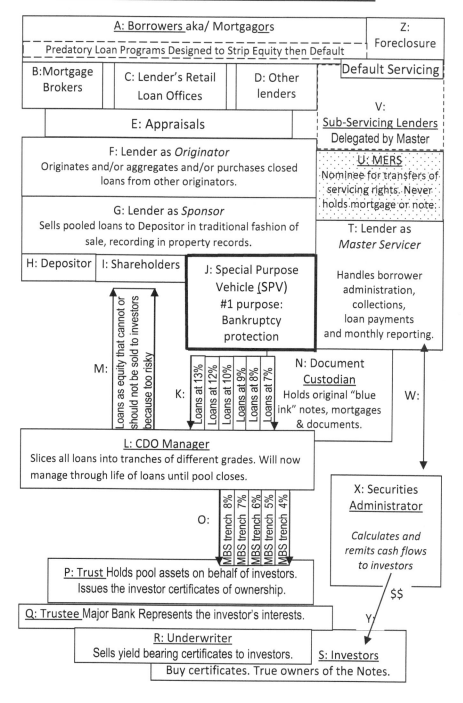

A: Borrowers aka/ Mortgagors	Z: Foreclosure
Predatory Loan Programs Designed to Strip Equity then Default	

Default Servicing

B:Mortgage Brokers	C: Lender's Retail Loan Offices	D: Other lenders

V:
Sub-Servicing Lenders
Delegated by Master

E: Appraisals

U: MERS
Nominee for transfers of servicing rights. Never holds mortgage or note.

F: Lender as *Originator*
Originates and/or aggregates and/or purchases closed loans from other originators.

G: Lender as *Sponsor*
Sells pooled loans to Depositor in traditional fashion of sale, recording in property records.

T: Lender as *Master Servicer*

Handles borrower administration, collections, loan payments and monthly reporting.

H: Depositor	I: Shareholders	J: Special Purpose Vehicle (SPV) #1 purpose: Bankruptcy protection

M: Loans as equity that cannot or should not be sold to investors because too risky

K: Loans at 13% | Loans at 12% | Loans at 10% | Loans at 9% | Loans at 8% | Loans at 7%

N: Document Custodian
Holds original "blue ink" notes, mortgages & documents.

W:

L: CDO Manager
Slices all loans into tranches of different grades. Will now manage through life of loans until pool closes.

O: MBS trench 8% | MBS trench 7% | MBS trench 6% | MBS trench 5% | MBS trench 4%

X: Securities Administrator

Calculates and remits cash flows to investors

P: Trust Holds pool assets on behalf of investors. Issues the investor certificates of ownership.

$$

Q: Trustee Major Bank Represents the investor's interests.

Y:

R: Underwriter
Sells yield bearing certificates to investors.

S: Investors
Buy certificates. True owners of the Notes.

Foreclosure Discovery in the SPV Presents Special Challenges

In the process of borrower discovery in a foreclosure case, this area of Swaps and CDOs is critical to ascertaining undisclosed financial profits the NRM Lenders have made using the borrower and their mortgage as a product for profit, designed to default and foreclose in the end. Therefore, it is important to understand how NRM Lenders make money in the face of alleging they are losing money in foreclosure.

Ownership can be proven, not just by possession of the current originally transferred note, but by who is paying for the insurance against default of the borrower. In foreclosure of the type addressed in this book, the Investors (S) are the owners of the mortgages, not the NRM Lenders claiming to be owners and submitting original notes into court from an old transaction that took place two or more sales ago. In keeping with that, the Investors (S) make insurance payments under the default swaps.

It is critical to determine if the Investors (S) have been paid on the presumed mortgage loss of an individual borrower. Investors may carry additional separate insurance against underlying mortgage default or loss, in addition to the credit default swaps serving as additional insurance. The financial calculation on the borrower's behalf involves ascertaining to what extent the investor has been paid as this affects the borrower's financial claims as an offset in the form of defensive recoupment in a case.

On the one hand it is important to learn to what extent investors have received insurance payments on the defaulted loan. On the other it is important to calculate the hidden profits earned by the NRM Lenders.

The credit default swaps present both scenarios.
- Profits to the NRM Lenders from selling and reselling synthetic credit default swaps over and over.
- Insurance to the Investors when an underlying mortgage(s) default or experience a downgrading of credit.

A swap does not require a default to pay out; it can pay out as the result of the underlying asset having its credit downgraded.

Discovery investigation may also include an additional underlying factor to consider in the swap agreement, prepayment. The event in which a borrower in the pool may refinance their mortgage and pay off the existing mortgage. This can result in an adjustment of the swap derivative. The Depositor (H) is relegated by most pooling and servicing agreements to deliver or cause to be delivered, a Prepayment Charge Schedule to the Master Servicer and Trustee on the closing date.

This prepayment charge schedule includes:
1. The mortgage loan identifying number
2. A code indicating the prepayment charge
3. The date on which the first monthly payment was due
4. The terms of the prepayment charge
5. The original stated balance of the loan.
6. The stated principal balance of the loan as of the cut-off date.

The Depositor (H) is involved with assessing the credit risk of the underlying mortgages before they are tranched into groups by the CDO Manager.

Profits in credit default swaps include any net swap payments, premiums and any swap termination payments made by the swap provider. Refer to the documentation of the particular mortgage pool for the details and terms. If synthetic credit default swaps that facilitate selling and reselling the same underlying assets over and over again are discovered, these profits should be included in borrower offset accounting.

If mortgage borrowers default, the investors still get paid.

This is a critical issue to understand because in foreclosure the investors are the owners of the mortgages. The NRM Lenders are walking away in many cases with the entire or nearly entire foreclosure amount received from the sale of assets. It is critical to determine if the investors have been paid on the presumed mortgage loss of an individual borrower. Investors carry separate insurance against loss and there are also credit default swaps serving as additional insurance. It is critical to the financial calculation on the borrower's behalf to know exactly to what extent the investor has been paid as this may affect the equity doctrine (fairness to the parties) that a judge applies in a case.

Ratings Agencies
No discussion of CDOs or Swaps or even the meltdown crisis would be complete without touching on the rating agencies such as Standard and Poor's, Moody's and Fitch. Many of the investors in the aftermarket sales of the Swaps and CDOs are large companies, pension trusts, insurance companies, mutual funds and banks. Many personal retirement and savings were therefore hinged on these investments. Governments, industry and private sector invested in the mortgage pools and derivative aftermarket securities, but everyone was affected in the Meltdown Crisis of 2008 and its aftermath.

The ratings agencies were always counted on to be independent and objective third parties whose analysts determined the value of the rated assets using standardized principals of accounting and asset valuation.

As soon as wholesale default of mortgages began to sweep the mortgage backed asset pools, it became apparent that the ratings agencies had also succumbed to greed and deception. The way mortgage pool ratings worked in securitization was the same way that the legal and accounting and other parts of the whole worked, payment on completion. From the earliest days of syndicated securitization, the model was the same, any service provider, accounting, legal, or ratings agency, was paid one fee if the deal closed, and a much lesser or no fee if it didn't. This was the modus operandi that bred high levels of competition among vendor peer groups. In other words, one company was extremely aggressive to keep business from a competitor. This was the same in the accounting, legal and ratings agency areas where competition is fierce.

Institutions may only invest in certain grades of assets. For example, BBB and above to AAA. The highest ratings translated to the lowest risk and the buyers received a lower cash flow for them. Under a certain category, say BBB for instance, certain fund managers were not even able to invest in the assets. For instance Pension Funds whose members, employees and contributors required a portfolio of less risk even if it produced less return. Preservation of retirement capital for example is more important than aggressive growth strategies and risks that mutual funds and aggressive growth funds might be willing to assume. Money market funds, where a lot of cash is kept in securities trading accounts are also restricted to the ratings they may invest in.

Whether the ratings agencies simply misunderstood the underlying assets, or they purposefully fell victim to the greed factor and didn't want to sit by while the competition churned out the highest ratings out there, the coveted AAA, the fact is, the ratings agencies made a mistake. Rating poor and mediocre mortgage borrowers pooled together in predatory loans destined to default on a predictable timeline was unfair, deceptive and misleading. While they lined their pockets with revenues, everyone counting on their integrity lost money depending on them to be honest and have integrity. No one guessed the ratings agencies would succumb to payment greed. Hindsight indicates this is, unfortunately true. It is just a matter of time until they are held accountable. The NRM Lenders used bankruptcy remote vehicles, as this section illustrates. It appears that the ratings agencies did not structure any such interim entities. This would have alerted investors to problems. The fact the ratings agencies signed off on their corporation's names indicated financial responsibility and made investors more comfortable.

One of the things that can get exposed in forensic analysis is the standard Conflicts of Interest section of disclosures. Not including the fact that the agencies were paid by the NRM Lender issuers of the CDOs and Swaps, a huge conflict of interest, may certainly be held as deception.

The Securities Exchange Act of 1934 granted certain credit rating agencies the coveted Nationally Recognized Statistical Rating

Organization (NRSRO) [7]status. It appears there are currently ten companies that have the coveted registration granted to them.

1. A.M. Best Company, Inc.
2. DBRS Ltd.
3. Egan-Jones Rating Company
4. Fitch, Inc.Japan Credit Rating Agency, Ltd.
5. LACE Financial Corp
6. Moody's Investors Service, Inc
7. Rating and Investment Information, Inc.
8. Realpoint LLC
9. Standard & Poor's Ratings Services

It is pertinent to note that there is an SEC Report [8] issued July 8, 2008 that summarized SEC examinations begun in August 2007 of Fitch, Moody's and Standard and Poor's to "review their role in the recent turmoil in the subprime mortgage related securities markets", more specifically mortgage backed securities and CDOs. One of the findings of the commission staff on page one is *"the rating agencies did not always document significant steps in the ratings process -- including the rationale for deviations from their models and for rating committee actions and decisions -- and they did not always document significant participants in the ratings process;"*. There are other significant issues. Perhaps they simply did not understand the process.

CREDIT DEFAULT SWAPS

The credit default swap cash flow, the premiums paid by the Investors, inures to the benefit of the NRM Lenders. The operation is critical to the hidden profits area of the NRM Lenders. It is magical in a way, because much of the overall transactional profits are manufactured here, via entities that for bankruptcy protection have no real assets, employees or actual business locations, and essentially disappear once the transaction is complete. Due to the simultaneous transactional nature of the enterprise, the entire asset structure goes in and out with simultaneous signing of agreements and closings. Thus, there is no corporation to chase, no entity to visit and no employees to depose or question.

---

[7] See http://www.sec.gov/divisions/marketreg/ratingagency.htm

Creation of the credit default swap transactions that are used to enhance the credit of the underlying mortgages include the creation of a Swap Trust enterprise owned by the NRM Lender and Origination parties and counterparties as Shareholders (I). None of the profits in this area endure to the Investors (S) in the Trust (P) enterprise of mortgages. Essentially this becomes an Issuer Trust within the Investor Trust. This aspect of the Issuer exclusively enjoying the financial income from the Swap premiums received by the Investors (S) can be confusing when reading about it in the Pooling and Servicing Agreement (PSA)

The Special Purpose Vehicle's (SPV) comes in to the transaction with no assets. It will develop a capital structure based upon the pooled mortgages it receives and the value created in enhancing the credit and repackaging these mortgages into groups (tranches) that will be sold to the investor Trust. The credit enhancement to raise tranche credit ratings will be provided utilizing Credit Default Swaps (Swaps). Ratings agencies such as Standard & Poor's, Moody's, and Fitch, who rate bond style investments (tranched mortgages included) provide ratings on the tranche slices in the form of AAA down to B and Unrated.

In this book, "up-tranching", refers to this form of credit enhancement. A higher credit rating means the issuer can sell at lower interest yields because the buyers (the Investors (S)) are willing to accept fewer yields on higher rated bonds. This translates into tremendous profits for the issuer. In this way, 8% loans of B rated mortgage borrowers can be up-tranched and sold as AAA rated debt requiring the issuer to pay only 4% cash flow. In this example a $300,000 mortgage at 8% can be sold for $600,000 paying only 4% to Investors.

NRM Lenders in the securitization process like to refer to excess spreads, alleging that the difference between the higher interest being received from the mortgages is in excess of the lower interest being paid to the investors, minus fees and such. This is purposefully misleading because in the up-tranching model this excess spread is capitalized into profits for the NRM Lenders. It is not passed on as received to the investors in the pool, at least not in the amounts received initially. Discovery analysis of the underlying mortgages, cross referenced with the pooled certificates and everything else in between must be undertaken by an entity who knows where to look for profits and real costs. To complicate this, NRM Lenders have created entities which materialize and then basically evaporate, making the process of forensic discovery all the more difficult.

The swap agreements provide insurance to the investor Trust (P) that in case the underlying mortgages default or in some cases their credit ratings are altered, the investors will be paid off. In exchange, the Trust (P) on behalf of the investors is buying this insurance and pays premiums on an ongoing basis.

The swaps show the additional revenue to the Originating NRM Lender wearing the Depositor "hat" and to what extent the investor has received swap insurance benefits on the borrower's loan.

Basically, the two swap counterparties, buyer and seller; agree to exchange streams of income from cash flows against other streams, more commonly referred to as the swap "legs". It is important to examine the Swap Agreement which defines the cash flows and dates when premiums are to be paid and how they are calculated.

The calculation, for simplicities sake, is based on the loan face amounts used to calculate the payments (sometimes referred to as the notional amount), a non-esoteric variable such as one widely published exchange rate such as the London Interbank Offered Rate (LIBOR) for example; and a stream of cash flow.

Swaps tie in to the Synthetic Collateralized Debt Obligations. The swaps can be unfunded. That means essentially that the counterparties can earn their profits or losses without ever having to put up the funds representing the security of the insured amounts, in cash or collateral. Swaps are among the most widely traded finance contracts.

In the foreclosure case, it is appropriate for the borrower's attorney to obtain a copy of the Swap Agreement, sometimes called the Interest Rate Swap Agreement. This will define the parties to the transaction who will act on behalf of an entity likely named something like the "supplemental interest trust", and the swap provider. The agreement will provide for Net Swap Payments and Swap Termination Payments to be paid, providing the method and process together with schedules, confirmations and other agreements relating to the swap.

The use of the phraseology and the parties is misleading and may confuse the uninitiated that the profits of these swaps are part of the investor's Trust, the one that owns the mortgage loans. That is not the case. Examination of the typical pooled mortgage transaction will show that the investor's claims of ownership specifically exclude this trust within a trust. The cash flow from the swap belongs to the issuer.

The "supplemental interest trust" is NOT the investor trust. It is just another way the Originating NRM Lender as Shareholder (I) and the Depositor (H) make profits it can pass on as payments to the NRM Lender as Sponsor (G) or Originator (F). What's more, in examining the swap documentation, an experienced forensic mortgage loan analyst can use the information gained in the process to determine if the loans have been sold multiple times using the unfunded and synthetic aspects.

While some may never have heard of Swaps, it is important to know that at the end of 2006, the Bank for International Settlements (BIS) who publishes statistics on the Over the Counter derivatives market, estimated that there were over $415 trillion US dollars worth on the market. That is more than eight times the entire world's gross national product. Nearly $300 trillion were interest rate swaps.

Obviously, $300 trillion of loans, some six times the world's gross product, are not in existence in their face amounts (the notional amount) so it can be deduced that multiple sales of actual mortgages takes place in order to get to this amount. The protagonists in this process are the Depositor (H) and the CDO Manager (L). This phenomenon is at the basis of the meltdown of 2008 and collapse of financial giants like Bear Stearns and Merrill Lynch, which will be discussed at the end of this section.

Typically, all the transaction calculation information is published in the Pooling and Servicing Agreement. For example, you will find the swap's notional amount defined, the rate such as LIBOR, the swap provider, and trigger events with termination payment definitions, termination prices and transfer instructions etc.

It is pertinent to know if the Originating NRM Lender, wearing the Depositor (H) hat or another hat such as a Shareholder (I) in the transaction, or as swap counterparty, is receiving premiums from the Trust investors on a regular published schedule. For example, in a one billion dollar trust, a one percent a month start rate payment is ten million dollars ($10,000,000) a month. As time goes by the percentage goes up, indicating an increased risk of default. This runs counter to conventional mortgage thinking that shows the risk of default goes down as the borrower pays their mortgage over years. For example, it is not surprising to find the swap premium interest rate going up to three percent and even five percent or more as time goes by.

To unravel the mystery of Swaps one needs to examine their history and basic aspects.

Swap History and the Basics
Swap contracts are a phenomenon created in the early 1980's and have been attributed to various people and entities. Whoever created them, the fact is, they are a major financial vehicle.

There are numerous kinds of swaps in the finance industry. The basic swap types are commodity, credit, currency, equity and interest. The credit swap is the one pertinent to this discussion, more accurately described as credit default swaps. This is a complex area of finance to understand comprehensively because there are many types of swaps within the basic types. However, to understand the credit default swap basics is a much easier task.

The swap is basically an agreement between two or more parties called counterparties. The party who purchases the swap, the buyer, receives protection in case the underlying assets default in their coupon payments. The seller guarantees the creditworthiness of the underlying assets. The result is a "perceived" insurance policy that seems to further support the underlying asset's credit worthiness.

"Perceived" because in many cases the across the board devaluation of the swap collateralized assets precipitated collapse and not payoffs by insurance. However, the promise was there. The investors paid swap "insurance" premiums to the Issuer so that in case of mortgage default investors would receive the full mortgage payoff amount if the borrowers defaulted.

COLLATERALIZED DEBT OBLIGATIONS (CDOs)

Collateralized Debt Obligations (CDOs) are Asset Backed Securities (ABSs) in a structured credit financial product. They basically hold assets as collateral and sell groups of cash flow from these assets, packaged in "classes" to investors. These classes are called "tranches" and are rated according to the underlying credit of each borrower behind their particular mortgage in the tranche. Mortgages will be grouped by the level of security of the underlying asset in the "tranche".

Senior tranches being the most secure with ratings of AAA, stepping down to the mezzanine tranches that are rated from AA, A, BBB, down to BB, and then to unrated Equity tranches at the lowest level where a rating is not possible because underlying borrower credit does not meet even the minimum standards for a rating.

The lower rated tranches compensate for the higher risk of default by offering higher coupon interest rates to the Investors (S). The lowest level Equity tranches may not be *able* to be sold because their risk is so high. The process of up-tranching (enhancing) borrower credit will provide payment of all mortgages plus profits. Lenders have no risk on any mortgage as a lender because they are paid in full by the investors for the mortgages when the pool is created.

NRM Lenders may also receive the highest risk Equity tranche mortgages as part of their shareholder profit in the Depositor (H). The Equity tranche can then be held as a high return asset by the participating lenders who organized the mortgages and securities themselves, as well as a perk asset to other parties responsible for selling and managing the investor side of the pooled transaction.

In this case over collateralized debt obligations refers to CDOs that are sold and resold using the same mortgages, not the situation where the lowest rated mortgages in the pool are in excess of and exceed the rated tranches.

From their beginnings in the late 1980's CDOs have proved important funding mediums for fixed income assets. NRM subprime Lenders simply put their own spin on them, to the eventual detriment of all.

The CDO process is intended to be fully understood only by the initiate few and certainly not by borrowers, attorneys, judges, congress, investors, their loan officers, account representatives, politicians, the media, or regulators. Because of that, lenders can operate hidden profit centers right under the nose of the regulatory agencies and get away with it.

When the ripple effect of the underlying mortgage defaults collapsed the markets, lenders were not subject to Congressional hearings in 2008 to get taxpayer bailouts like the Savings & Loans were in the 1980's. The complications of CDO and Swap derivatives structure proved too complicated for Congress to understand, which served to protect the NRM Lenders and attract bailout funds to such insurance giants as AIG.

Collateralized Debt Obligations (CDOs) can refer to any debt backed by assets. Airplanes, equipment, account receivables, etc. In regards to mortgages, Collateralized Mortgage Obligations (CMOs) is a more appropriate term but because mortgages are also assets, Collateralized Debt Obligations (CDOs) also applies and is more commonly used.

When a specific mortgage asset is pledged, this is referred to as a "Cash CDO", meaning the party that paid the cash now owns the underlying assets outright. Cash CDOs own the individual loans or bonds and are not suitable to reselling the same mortgages over and over again to other mortgage pools because the buyers will require the original blue ink signed note and mortgage with proper transfers and assignments noted or attached. This is not the case with "Synthetic CDOs".

Synthetic CDO's

Significant to NRM Lender continued profits is the hidden ability to continue to sell mortgages in the form of synthetic credit default swaps and collateralized debt obligations to others and earn profits on them.

In order to sell and resell the same mortgages over and over, NRM Lenders made use of "Synthetic CDOs". These are basically artificial pools of mortgages designed to replicate the security of real underlying mortgages. In short, smoke and mirrors.

Hybrid CDOs

Hybrids are blends of Synthetic CDOs and real tangible Cash CDOs.

Swap Counterparties

The plan of reaping upfront and ongoing profits utilizes Swap Counterparties to earn additional money on interest arbitrages and spreads. The beauty of this is that Swap Counterparties have no "real" money in senior synthetic CDO tranche derivative credit default swaps. They only have the risk of "paying on credit defaults" if and when the investments collapse. "If" is used in documentation describing risk. In retrospect, it was really "when".

CDOS, SWAPS AND THE MELTDOWN OF 2008

Rudimentary understanding of Swaps and Collateralized Debt Obligations will also answer a lot of questions about the collapse of financial markets and the Meltdown of 2008.

In response to the lack of continued genuine original borrower mortgage product, NRM Lenders created their own Synthetic CDO Derivatives to fully support the NRM Lenders' own portions of investor pools, instead of coming up with the actual new mortgages from the limited supply of borrowers.

Ingenious NRM Lenders began to simply sell these Synthetic CDO Derivatives to investors. Raking in billions without actually having to perform loan origination, which is a big job to be sure. NRM Lenders faced with not having to originate fresh mortgages, which takes time, were elated.

Imagine sitting at a cash register all day long ringing up billion dollar sales and handing out bags of air that buyers thought were bags of diamonds and gold. This is a case of the truth being stranger than fiction. If it weren't history at this point, no one would believe it. In fact, even faced with the undisputable evidence, most people still don't want to believe it.

According to BIS, as mentioned earlier, there were a few hundred trillion (with a "t") of collateralized debt obligations and swap derivatives traded in the financial marketplaces (for example, the Over the Counter market), an amount equal to about six times the entire world's gross product at the time of this writing. Certainly this is a far greater amount than there are mortgages or other assets to actually back up these derivatives. In many cases the derivatives are cross collateralizing the same assets, yet selling them as bona fide investments. In a market where the entire swath of mortgages underlying the assets begins defaulting, as we had in the Meltdown of 2008, the entire value of these "smoke and mirror" derivatives reaches their true values, meaning they implode and become comparatively worthless. For example, a couple trillion of real assets cannot support a few hundred trillion of swap derivative investments claiming to be backed up with real assets even though they were cross collateralized.

In other words, say that one home and one borrower were pledged to secure three hundred investors counting on the underlying security of the mortgage and property to make them whole. Each of these three hundred investors put up enough money to essentially buy that mortgage secured by that one home. Through massive devaluation of the asset upon realization of this over collateralization, when discovered, the entire three hundred resales now plummet in value to equal the value of the one underlying mortgage and home, hence pennies or fractions of a penny on the dollar. Now the two hundred ninety nine investments over the one that really owns something tangible underneath see the value of their particular holdings collapse. When they look around, everyone else holding similar over collateralized synthetic investments are also experiencing the wholesale devaluation and collapse of value as well. Now investor sentiment and fears create a psychology of panic, no one is buying, everyone is trying to dump what they now come to realize were highly overvalued, over rated and over collateralized "junk" bonds. Trading activity on the upside ceases.

When the Federal Reserve Board, the Securities and Exchange Commission, and the Federal Accounting Standards Board understood this, they caused the accounting rules to be changed from promised value of returns alleged to be paid over time, to Mark to Market value. This single event triggered the Meltdown 0f 2008. Promised value involved assuming that a bond would pay itself off in the long run at its face value, which would be impossible because one mortgage could not pay off the equivalent of three hundred mortgages.

However, during the securitization heyday between 2000 and 2006 for example, before the bottom fell out, this type of activity was normal, accepted and commonplace.

For those interested, within one calendar quarter (three months), of the mark to market valuation standards being imposed, investment banking firms, banks, insurance companies and those who had massive holdings of these toxic investments began to collapse en masse. The purchasers must have felt these were good investments. This indicates that the market did not understand them.

An obvious interjection here would be to conclude that the Trusts, the investors of these inflated swap derivatives and collateralized debt obligations and the corporations purchasing them would have been well advised to hire a credible mortgage analysis firm to assess the true value of these toxic assets prior to jumping with both feet into them. The penalty in many cases for these companies that did not consider mortgage analysis as insurance and prevention of loss, turned billions of dollars in stock value into bankruptcy, failure and collapse to mere fractions of their former corporate value. What makes this even worse is the number of Americans whose asset base also crumbled, as they

118

watched shares they owned in these companies collapse along with their lives and dreams.

The following covers the actual processes behind selling and reselling the same mortgages over and over again in Mortgage Backed Securities (MBS) Synthetic CDOs and MBS Credit Default Swap transactions.

The synthetic MBS Swap transaction attempts to replicate the cash flow patterns of the mortgage transactions, without providing the mortgage notes on a cash basis to support the assets. A synthetic asset basically "portrays" the characteristics of the mortgage terms and payments without the mortgage itself.

The basics of the MBS Swap transactions are to essentially insure the Trust investors purchasing the mortgage pool assets against loss from defaults and in some cases credit downgrades. The investors essentially pay an interim party an ongoing stream of income for this "insurance". This insurance premium represents additional profits. What's more, the swaps may also be synthetic, meaning they can be sold without the direct underlying mortgage assets (original notes) being received and in this manner facilitate the same selling and reselling.

Cap Rate Cash Flow
The investor mortgage backed pool certificates are typically issued as debentures, meaning bonds. These CDO "bond" type derivatives were priced on at cap cash flow. Cap meaning capitalization for short. It is the total dollar amount paid to the investors each year, divided by the total investor purchase price of the pooled mortgages. As long as the investors received their promised yield, everything was fine. The Meltdown of 2008 insured this didn't last long.

CDOs were designed to be complicated.
In other words, when the pool has all its mortgages in place and the borrowers' credit that was originally poor has been upgraded, the Synthetic CDOs can be packaged and sold. Since the original notes

are not required, no property recording takes place. In that way, no one knows for sure if what they are buying is really owned because there is no record of the proper transfer. So now, the Synthetic CDOs can be sold and resold over and over again, not at the face amount of the mortgage but at the inflated price represented by the lower required cash flow payouts to investors being much below what the borrowers are paying in mortgage payments. Remember that in this example, the $800 million in mortgages was selling to investors for $1.2 billion. The synthetics are being sold at the $1.2 billion price. To create the illusion of additional security, the packagers allege the transaction includes claims into other similar investment vehicles. That may be true but when the value of the claimed interests is worthless because they are based on smoke and mirrors, as they proved to be, this was false security.

The benefits to NRM Lenders and packagers of Synthetic CDOs can be extended even further. The Synthetic CDOs could essentially be margined for the leverage to buy even more. This means they put up a percentage in cash and leveraged the rest with loans, similar to buying stock on margin.

When the Securities and Exchange Commission (SEC) decided to follow the advice of the Financial Accounting Standards Board (FASB) and issue orders to mark the assets to market instead of carrying them at the arbitrarily inflated values which had no relationship to the real assets underlying them, Meltdown 2008 occurred.

The SEC Triggered Meltdown 2008
The SEC and FASB govern what accounting methods are used for their constituents. The simple act of changing the valuation model to Mark to Market (MTM) caused the CDO values to plummet to near worthless levels once borrowers began to default on their loans. Add this to the 2007 repeal of the "up-tick rule", which required investors to wait for an up-tick in a stock prior to taking a short position, and stocks were able to plummet unsupported as well. The combinations of these two SEC actions triggered the meltdown.

Bank Collapse

But that wasn't all, the banking entities who owned these investments in the billions and trillions were required to maintain capital ratios (ratios of capital to its risk-weighted assets). The devaluation of the CDO assets meant that the banks needed to have more cash on hand to meet their capital requirements. The banks started dumping any assets that could quickly generate cash, which meant stocks and bonds. This action drove down values of these stocks and bonds and forced margin calls on many investors who were buying on margin. As a result these investors had to dump holdings to generate cash to meet the margin calls. The result was that the markets tanked. Banks collapsed and the FDIC and Federal Reserve stepped in.

Market Collapse Presents Bank Profiteering via Acquisitions.

NRM Lenders, unlike regulated banks, can and did accumulate war chests from the actions leading up to the Meltdown of 2008, simply mimicking what their predecessors did in the Great Depression Era. Massive consolidation ensued as companies were bought for pennies on the dollar occurred.

An Aside, Classic Banking Stock Market Manipulation

The challenge to the NRM Lenders was to make untold riches using one simple piece of knowledge they had that no one else had. Namely, they knew when the mortgages would begin defaulting. They knew this because they originated, bought and underwrote the individual mortgages.

Abolishment of the Up-Tick Rule

The SEC had abolished the up-tick rule, established in the Great Depression to prevent exactly the same collapse of the stock market and profiteering of those who understood short selling into a collapsing market. Short selling for profit is borrowing stocks from brokerages at the highs, selling them at the highs, then returning the shares back purchased at pennies on the dollar with one obvious perk, the one who performed these trades kept the difference as profit. The other perk was not so obvious, control. When you can buy one hundred million dollars of equity in a company for one million dollars, and make profit in the process, you can acquire controlling interests that pay you, rather than cost you. The type of forensics to discover this involves forensic accounting. It is a very time consuming, difficult and costly enterprise. This is a specialty available at many large accounting firms. Borrowers and their attorneys are not going to realistically be in the position to discover these profits exactly. One needs the resources of Attorneys General and Congressionally funded investigative committees (large amounts of tax payer dollars) to do this.

Building a Diversified NRM Lender War Chest

Stocks and bonds are not the only things NRM Lenders can buy with their fortunes; they can also buy real Asset Backed Securities (ABSs) from other banks. These can be airplanes, heavy equipment and account receivables, all at deep discounts as banks scramble to meet their Federal Reserve deposit requirements in the same fashion as investors.

War chests full of acquired cash equivalent assets, stocks paid for in full, cash positions in money market accounts, accounts easily converted to cash that pay interest such as bonds and Guaranteed Investment Contracts (GICs) can be used to swoop in and pick up bargain priced blue chip assets. Once the recovery takes place, these will be worth fortunes. This banking and securities opportunity has not existed since the Great Depression because our government locked it down in the 1933 with the Banking Act.

The Masquerade: Lenders as Victims in Foreclosure

When it came time to implement the exit strategy and move into the Foreclosure (Z) profit area, it was and is important for the lenders to be seen as victims of borrowers who were overreaching in a hot real estate market, not the orchestrators of the inevitable collapse.

Mark to Market: Trigger One of the Meltdown of 2008

The Mark to Market (MTM) accounting standard was a critical element to initiating the collapse. Initially, lenders value the derivative investments as long term mortgage holdings at full value. Eventually, just as the mass of loans begin to default, lenders simply change the valuation of these derivatives into trading assets which will actually have no value considering massive defaults. This action will precipitate the meltdown crisis and catapult the syndicating lenders into the Foreclosure (Z) phase of operations.

As long term holdings, lender derivative investments are classified under Securities and Exchange Commission (SEC) and Financial Accounting Standards Board (FASB) regulations that value them at about the full face value of the mortgages. Not so when Mark to Market (MTM) is used. Adopting the MTM method of accounting initiated the side benefit of picking up banks, investment firms, and company stock for pennies on the dollar. To instigate the collapse enter the Foreclosure (Z) phase. Simply change the value of asset holdings to come under the Mark to Market rules. When it turns out the values are based on mortgages that are defaulting system wide, the assets will be trading for pennies on the dollar. The investment banking firms and insurance companies that underwrote the mortgage pools will now be faced with a massive sell off that they will not possibly catch up with.

Mark to Market Triggers the Foreclosure Exit Strategy
This is also the syndicating lenders primary getaway plan. The lenders will put the blame on mortgage brokers and greedy borrowers who lied to qualify for loans they couldn't afford. The lenders will have trillions in assets of hard properties in Foreclosure (Z) as well as whatever side assets they have accumulated in cash. Lenders and individuals in the "know" can then buy up the banks, investment houses and blue chip companies for pennies on the dollar via a stock market that is crashing.

Masquerade as Victim of Meltdown 2008, Not Perpetrator of It.
Lenders will not take the "heat", the "meltdown" will appear to be the result of "over margining". While they are receiving regular payments as "insurance" against defaults, the swap counterparties will be living high. When the defaults start occurring in the hundreds of billions, the lenders' swap counterparties will crash from margin calls on the derivatives. The huge entities that partner and cooperate with the syndicating non-regulated subprime lenders like Bear Stearns, Merrill Lynch, AIG and others will be brought to their knees.

123

Collateralized Debt Obligations Manager

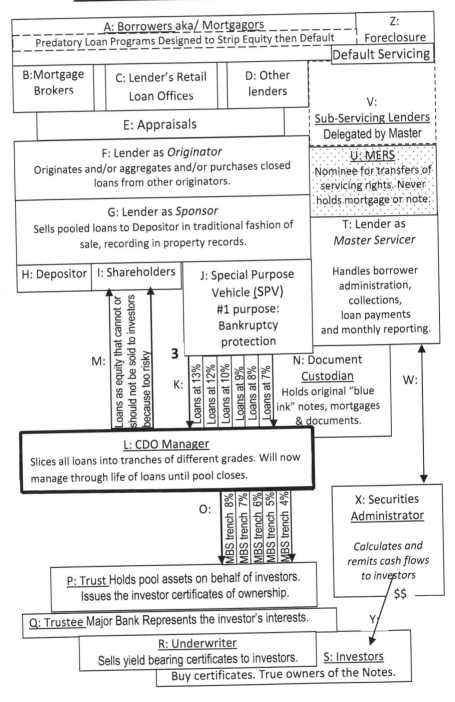

A: Borrowers aka/ Mortgagors
Predatory Loan Programs Designed to Strip Equity then Default

Z: Foreclosure

Default Servicing

B:Mortgage Brokers

C: Lender's Retail Loan Offices

D: Other lenders

V: Sub-Servicing Lenders Delegated by Master

E: Appraisals

F: Lender as *Originator*
Originates and/or aggregates and/or purchases closed loans from other originators.

U: MERS
Nominee for transfers of servicing rights. Never holds mortgage or note.

G: Lender as *Sponsor*
Sells pooled loans to Depositor in traditional fashion of sale, recording in property records.

T: Lender as *Master Servicer*

H: Depositor

I: Shareholders

J: Special Purpose Vehicle (SPV) #1 purpose: Bankruptcy protection

Handles borrower administration, collections, loan payments and monthly reporting.

M: Loans as equity that cannot or should not be sold to investors because too risky

3

K: Loans at 13% Loans at 12% Loans at 10% Loans at 9% Loans at 8% Loans at 7%

N: Document Custodian
Holds original "blue ink" notes, mortgages & documents.

W:

L: CDO Manager
Slices all loans into tranches of different grades. Will now manage through life of loans until pool closes.

O: MBS trench 8% MBS trench 7% MBS trench 6% MBS trench 5% MBS trench 4%

X: Securities Administrator
Calculates and remits cash flows to investors

$$

P: Trust Holds pool assets on behalf of investors. Issues the investor certificates of ownership.

Q: Trustee Major Bank Represents the investor's interests.

Y:

R: Underwriter
Sells yield bearing certificates to investors.

S: Investors
Buy certificates. True owners of the Notes.

The Collateralized Debt Obligations (L) (CDO) Manager.

The CDO Manager is an individual, often working for a firm that specializes in creating and managing CDOs.

The job of the CDO Manager (L) is to accumulate the Underlying borrowers mortgage collateral (K) in the pool and then issue debt obligations (O) against that collateral. The debt obligations (O) are sliced up into "tranches" based on the different grades of underlying credit of the borrowers. The tranches are credit enhanced and sold to the investors in the Trust.

The CDO Manager (L) earns transactional fees both initially and over the life of the Trust. CDO Managers may also be investors and buy the lowest level credit tranches, unrated tranches and portfolios of defaulted loans (sometimes known as junk mortgage backed bonds) at a discount.

The CDO Manager has a complete list of the mortgages and credit ratings attached to them going in on the one side, and the details of the tranches (O) going out on the other. The CDO Manager also has the details of the Loans (M) that are given back to the Shareholders (I) in the form of equity that cannot or should not be sold to investors because they are too risky. The CDO Manager may also be aware of who the Shareholders (I) are.

The real job of the CDO Manager is credit enhancement. Turn the low grade mortgages into high grade securities and then sell them to investors at lower yields for profit, as detailed in the SPV section.

How this works is supposedly a big mystery, one the credit ratings agencies alleged to understand but in fact they didn't understand it at all. If they did, the AAA rated tranches would be rated B or unrated, as is now known in the aftermath of widespread defaults in the AAA and other tranche levels, that were supposed to be so highly rated.

In actuality the Credit Default Swaps which were based on smoke and mirrors, were alleged to further underlie the tranches as insurance which was outlined in the previous chapter.

The question of how much smoke and mirror value to add to the tranches to realize the superior AAA rating and maximize profit to the securitization process for the NRM Lenders, was given a formula so the credit agency analysts had something to go on. Just more fluff in the NRM Lender securitization model designed to mislead everyone.

In reality, the process is just as simple as is stated in this book. Originate the mortgages at as high a percentage rate as possible and then sell them at the lowest percentages possible to investors. Simply mark up the cost and back into the profits. Of course, that would not work if it was easily understood, so the NRM Lenders instituted a complex financial calculation formula that was difficult to understand.

The NRM Lender and CDO Manager understood; they performed their math like it is performed in this book. However the ratings agencies, which were the critical missing link, were given another approach. Eventually, if / when the ratings agencies were brought to task, they wouldn't really know what they were talking about.

Chapter 12

MERS® Exposed, Tool for Ownership Deception

MERS®, created by the NRM Lenders, has tricked many courts into believing MERS® is the owner of the properly transferred note and mortgage. Finally, courts across America have proven this false, but there is no penalty for trying to misrepresent this fact in a court of law, so borrowers' attorneys need to be very aware of the MERS® ruse.

MERS®, the Mortgage Electronic Registration System (MERS®) is an entity established by the mortgage banking industry to act as the nominee in the <u>transfer</u> of mortgage <u>servicing</u>. The ruse revolves around getting the court to believe MERS® is an owner in due course of the note and mortgage. MERS® registers loan *servicing transfers*, <u>not</u> true original ownership sales that include the original mortgage note and mortgage. In order not to be fooled, it is important to understand MERS®.

Standing to Foreclose is Based on Proper Evidence of Ownership. True sales must be registered in the appropriate county's land records in accordance with the pooling and servicing agreements. MERS® itself does not take possession of a note, original or otherwise. MERS® does not replace the traditional property clerk recording required for true note sale recording. It is now established at law in courts across America; MERS® does not have proper standing to foreclosure.

The challenge is to understand the use of MERS® and how this use has tricked so many courts into granting foreclosure improperly. MERS® has been used to literally put *millions* of borrowers into

127

MERS® Exposed, Tool for Ownership Deception

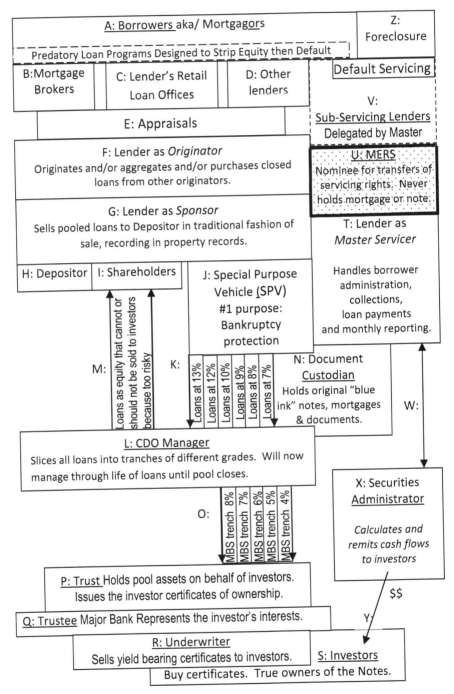

foreclosure, based upon misrepresented ownership. Unfortunately for those who have fallen victim in the past by improper standing to foreclosure, there is little that can be done after the fact. When presented with the MERS® ruse, one must confront it head on and with decisive evidence.

Company Background

MERS® is a corporation with common stock. The MERS® main data center is located in Texas. Serving as the "nominee" in all 50 U.S. States, MERS® has registered <u>servicers</u> of tens of millions of loans. Some reports allege more than 50,000,000 loans. Whatever the actual number is, it is a BIG number. However, this is servicing, NOT ownership.

The Nominee Clause Pertains to Loan Servicing, Not Ownership. Lenders use the "MERS® as nominee" clause in mortgages they originate to fraudulently assert MERS® is the real owner at the time of seeking summary judgment of foreclosure in court.

Many courts are aware of this frivolous misrepresentation. In Florida for instance, this sham has been outlawed in courts. **A look online at www.mersinc.org in MERS® rules will confirm <u>$10,000 per occurrence fines</u> to lender members that try these shenanigans in Florida.** However, lenders still try again and again because the risk of being caught red-handed in a MERS® ownership allegation does not bear any significant penalties. The worst a lender can expect is only a possible dismissal with the right to come back to court and try again. Until such time as courts dole out significant penalties, the misrepresentative and fraudulent MERS® claims of rightful current ownership of note and mortgage will still be made.

MERS® is simply a utilitarian tool to eliminate the paper mortgage transfer process in servicing loans. The mortgage banking industry claims MERS® promotes mortgage commerce by electronically registering the rights and interest other mortgage banks have in particular mortgage loans. MERS® simply records loan *servicing transfers* from one servicing lender to another servicing lender. Governmental agencies do not take exception to this because the servicing transfers are not ownership transfers and therefore do not incur transfer taxes in the same manner note and mortgage transfers do. If they were, then the traditional methods of property clerk recordings would have to be used.

In considering what law refers to as "standing" the right to bring a foreclosure case, courts, including appellate, have mandated the following:

1. Only the current holder of the note at the time of commencing the foreclosure action can properly prosecute the action.

2. Entry of a default judgment against a borrower is not appropriate where the lender's ownership is not ascertainable from the documentation submitted in support of the motion.

3. Many courts have repeatedly held that MERS® cannot prosecute foreclosure in its own name as nominee for the lender because it lacks ownership of the mortgage and note at the time the case is prosecuted. MERS® never owns the mortgage or note and is never in possession of it.

MERS® is a publically accessible registration system with online access for any party to find out who the registered servicer of a loan is, as long as the loan has a duly issued MERS® "MIN" mortgage identification number. This is an 18 digit identifier found on the face of a mortgage that MERS® is held as a nominee on, that can be used to search. All mortgages are not registered with MERS® as a nominee, so some loans may not have a MIN number. Searches on the MERS® **web site** can also be conducted using various other inputs such as borrower name, address, etc.

Anyone can find out the current loan servicer of a MERS® registered loan, online via the world wide web, instantly any time day or night. In foreclosure this is important because a loan may not show a recent servicing transfer anywhere else but on MERS®. This is important in order to make sure that the proper loan servicer is being contacted.

Anyone seeking to send a Qualified Written Request for information under Section 6 of the Real Estate and Settlement Procedures Act or interested in sending a rescission package or any correspondence to a loan servicer, will want to include the most recently recorded mortgage servicing entity in order to maintain consistent validity and conform with regulations.

MERS® empowers MERS® Ready trading partners, meaning mortgage banker, lending and loan servicing companies, to title trading partner employees working in the trading partner's company offices as Vice Presidents of MERS®. These folks, often secretaries and administrative assistants are empowered to <u>appear</u> as executives of MERS®, but which are actually employees of the member firm and not executives of the parent MERS ® Corporation.[8] MERS® acknowledges this relationship and publishes considerable documentation on their website www.mersinc.org. There are also a plethora of cases and over one hundred pages of Hon. Judge Jon Gordon's transcripts[9] on MERS® that illustrate and discuss dismissing nine cases of MERS® as sham pleadings. MERS® now prohibits certain claims in Florida with grave consequences for members who violate that.[10]

MERS® officially adopted their bankruptcy remote model in 1999. MERS® became approved by Moody's, Fitch, and Standard & Poor's and in 1999 participated as the nominee in Lehman's first AAA rated securitized mortgage pool. ($284 million).

MERS® is mentioned on mortgages because of the servicing requirements, but MERS® is never mentioned on the Notes because they are never true owners. This is the basis of MERS®

---

[8] Confirmed in the Business Procedures section of the MERS Procedures Handbook . The member "forms an integration team" in step one, and in step two sends "a list of certifying officers to the MERS Corporate Offices." At which point the member "attends a MERS online training session" which "trains your staff on the use of MERS". *MERS Procedures Manual – Release 18.0–6/8/09*

[9] 11th Judicial Circuit, Miami-Dade County, Florida; Civil Division Case 05-02425 CA 05; MERS v. Enzon Cabreara. Robert Brochin Esq., for MERS®. FL Bar # 0319661

[10] www.mersinc.org

not qualifying in court as the owner in a foreclosure action. Only the current owner of the note and mortgage at the time of commencing a foreclosure action may properly prosecute said action.

What MERS® Isn't:
The fact that so many Lenders have pulled the wool over so many courts' eyes misrepresenting MERS® ownership interests means a great many foreclosure defense attorneys are not clear on exactly the role MERS® plays and what MERS® is not and does not do.

MERS® is a "Nominee" ONLY. This means the <u>mortgage</u> security is <u>*registered*</u> to them for servicing transfer notice, but the <u>true ownership</u> and holder of the original "blue inked" copy of the mortgage and note, <u>IS HELD BY SOMEONE ELSE, SOME OTHER PARTY</u>. In a securitized transaction the owner is the investors of the pooled mortgages in the form of a Trust represented by a Trustee.

MERS® is not a party to the mortgage debt or instruments, except as nominee. Nominee means basically "holder". They have no interest at all, other than nominee. No legal or beneficial interest. No financial or other interest in seeing that the loan is repaid in whole or part. They don't care about payments, repayments, or anything. They don't get any payments, any rights, title or interest in the underlying property securing the loan. The borrower is not obligated in any way, and owes absolutely nothing to MERS®. The borrower has never and will never pay one thin dime to MERS® on account of MERS® being the nominee, other than a nominal registration fee.

MERS® never has any interaction with the borrower. MERS® is never named as a beneficiary of the promissory note, that "blue ink" signed promise to pay that details the terms of the mortgage. MERS® never took a loan application, originated mortgage loan documents, processed a loan or even had a phone conversation with the borrower. They don't have the licenses required, the employees or the wherewithal. They can't extend credit. MERS® does not originate loans *at all*.

MERS® doesn't service loans, does not buy servicing rights, does not sell servicing rights. MERS® never has contact with borrowers, doesn't collect even one payment, and doesn't issue as much as a single piece of paper to borrowers. MERS® is not an investor that would buy a loan and they therefore do not sell loans.

MERS® does not carry loans on their books, they don't care if the loan is current or in default, their corporate earnings are not going to be influenced in any way based upon collection, payment or default of any loan they in which they are acting as nominee. Ironically, MERS® is often initially named on the SAME SIDE as a Borrower in default facing a foreclosure lawsuit, so as to advise and include MERS® in the foreclosure action. That further evidences that no conflict exists between the borrower and MERS®, even when the loan is in default.

MERS® wouldn't actually keep any money from the sale of a foreclosed property, even if they received money. MERS® would be instantly required to remit all proceeds to the true ownership party in interest but this hypothetical occurrence is just that, it is not an occurrence taking place on a regular basis.

Put another way the MERS® "ruse" is a Lender attempting to foreclose asserting to the court that MERS® is indeed an owner holder of the mortgage and note. In that way, the NRM Lender lie can be perpetrated into fraud by asking the court to award replacement of the "lost" note so the servicing lender can get the borrower's home in foreclosure.

MERS® itself is not able to tell a court who the real beneficial owner is. In simply allowing any employee of an affiliated third party, such as a lender or servicer to be endowed as a V.P., of MERS®, MERS® itself, meaning the MERS ® Corporation, actually has no participation in a manner one would expect a traditional corporation to have. MERS ® Corporation never laid eyes on borrower documents.

This non-traditional MERS® V.P., employee never receives a cent of remuneration from **MERS® Corporation**, yet they can swear out false affidavits in MERS® name. The servicing lender instructs their MERS® V.P., lender's employee to "sign this". It is said that most lender's employees will sign anything to stay off the unemployment lines.

The courts have exposed MERS® for what it really is. Has MERS® suffered? Have they gone to jail? Have they been indicted? Nothing of the sort. They have been caught red handed. They have been forbidden to perpetrate the ownership sham in courts and states such as Florida. MERS® leaves no accounting trail, no recording required. The trail left by the MERS® ruse in court feigning ownership of the note and not being caught in the process has left millions of borrowers with eviction by foreclosure and NRM Lenders much richer for it.

The obvious benefit of MERS® is to simply track transfers of loan servicers. They are admittedly, via their own documentation, a bankruptcy remote entity, and since MERS® itself is not making the claims of fraudulent ownership, supposedly, they are not opening themselves to civil or criminal damages in the process. As a creation of the NRM Lenders and other banks, MERS® is paid a nominal fee of dollars per loan transaction registered. If they indeed have fifty million loans registered and changing hands, as has been bandied about the industry in statistics, it appears the company is successful simply doing what they were organized to do; monitor and register servicing and transfers of servicing rights between loan servicers.

Chapter 13

Lender Objectives in Court – 3 Diagrams

- ### Summary Judgment

- ### What Lenders Do NOT Want the Court to See

- ### What Lenders Want the Court To Believe.

- ### How Lenders Falsely Portray Themselves in Court

Lender Objectives in Court

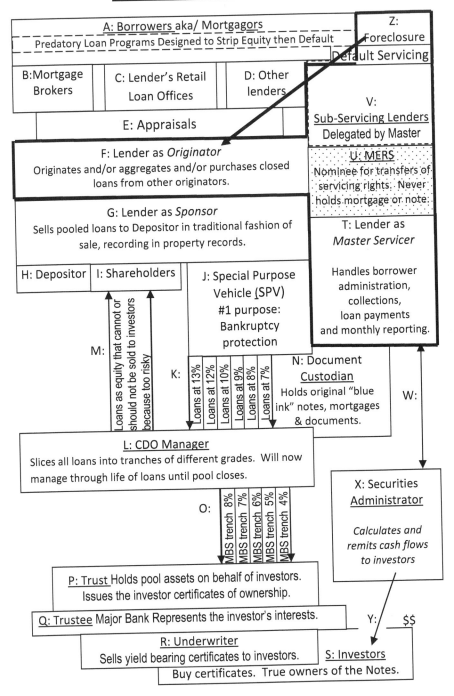

A: Borrowers aka/ Mortgagors
Predatory Loan Programs Designed to Strip Equity then Default

Z: Foreclosure
Default Servicing

B: Mortgage Brokers

C: Lender's Retail Loan Offices

D: Other lenders

E: Appraisals

V: Sub-Servicing Lenders Delegated by Master

F: Lender as _Originator_
Originates and/or aggregates and/or purchases closed loans from other originators.

U: MERS Nominee for transfers of servicing rights. Never holds mortgage or note.

G: Lender as _Sponsor_
Sells pooled loans to Depositor in traditional fashion of sale, recording in property records.

T: Lender as _Master Servicer_
Handles borrower administration, collections, loan payments and monthly reporting.

H: Depositor

I: Shareholders

J: Special Purpose Vehicle (SPV) #1 purpose: Bankruptcy protection

M: Loans as equity that cannot or should not be sold to investors because too risky

K: Loans at 13% | Loans at 12% | Loans at 10% | Loans at 9% | Loans at 8% | Loans at 7%

N: Document Custodian Holds original "blue ink" notes, mortgages & documents.

W:

L: CDO Manager
Slices all loans into tranches of different grades. Will now manage through life of loans until pool closes.

O: MBS trench 8% | MBS trench 7% | MBS trench 6% | MBS trench 5% | MBS trench 4%

X: Securities Administrator
Calculates and remits cash flows to investors

P: Trust Holds pool assets on behalf of investors. Issues the investor certificates of ownership.

Q: Trustee Major Bank Represents the investor's interests.

Y: $$

R: Underwriter
Sells yield bearing certificates to investors.

S: Investors
Buy certificates. True owners of the Notes.

• Lender Objectives in Court – Summary Judgment

The lender will attempt to win foreclosure by Motion for Summary Judgment. This is the process of a judge ruling, without a jury trial, in favor of one side based on the evidence submitted into the case or the lack of response or evidence submitted. In order to win by Summary Judgment one side will attempt to prove that there are no material facts in opposition to the claims and therefore no issues to be tried. Summary Judgment is the first target of the lender in foreclosure case in court.

Borrowers can lose to Summary Judgment by not responding to court actions properly or within the time frames allotted. The lender wants to eliminate any possibility of having to go through discovery, answer interrogatories and provide admissions to allegations by the borrower, their attorney or a mortgage analysis expert. The lender will persuade the court by making statements and supplying documentary evidence. Lender desperation to get Summary Judgment may result in false statements.

The foreclosure mill lender's attorneys often submit documents and make statements that are easily proven false in court by experts. Lenders want to be perceived as parties who have been wronged by irresponsible borrowers. The unfortunate reality of the situation is most borrowers and many attorneys do not know how to find the expert mortgage analysis firm which may be their only credible resource to fight back. Some borrowers' attorneys think that making allegations is enough. This is not generally the case. Surfing the Internet for a credible mortgage analysis source can be frustrating and counterproductive.

Typically, the servicing lender is the party seeking to foreclose and be awarded the property by the court in Summary Judgment. They will do and say almost anything to represent themselves as the traditional lender wronged by a borrower with financial troubles. The allegations NRM Lenders make are difficult for the uninitiated to see through. Courts are designed to believe sworn statements and evidence. Therefore the borrower's attorney must provide evidence, not allegations, that the statements made by the lender are false. Boiler plate lists acquired from blogs with template style allegations will not meet the level of evidence and discovery provided by a credible third party forensic mortgage analysis firm that qualifies to submit findings under the rules of evidence. Including this type and level of evidence as part a credible legal defense is the key to successful borrower attorney strategies.

Courts and presiding judges as well as court appointed mediators will look seriously at credible resources of indisputable evidence or requests that will be used by experts to clear up material issues. Borrowers or their attorneys may be too frugal to spend any money on critical outside third party evidentiary findings. Often this is because they do not have a strategy to win. Their strategy is simply to delay in the hopes of the borrower getting a loan modification. Many attorneys do not understand the strategy of winning against foreclosure. Hopefully this book will change that.

- **What Lenders Do NOT Want the Court To See**

NRM Lenders conceal at all costs, the evidences of being paid in full for the mortgage at closing by investors in the mortgage pool. Effectively the lender is acting as broker.

Lender's mortgage risk at that point evaporated. The lender does not have one thin dime in that mortgage going forward from that point.

Lender upgraded the borrower's credit, via "up-tranching" the loan in securitization for hundreds of thousands of dollars, or more, in hidden profits. These hidden profits are created for the lender as a shareholder in the Hidden Profit Areas (see section of same name) involving the Depositor (H), Special Purpose Vehicle (J) (SPV) and CDO Manager (L).

Lender resold the same loan over and over again in synthetic collateralized debt obligation derivatives and default credit swaps. This is a reason why Lenders are reluctant to produce the original note, but it masks the major reason. It could be forced buy back of the defective mortgage from the Trust of Investors at fully marked up face value.

Lenders desperately try to hide the note and mortgage transfers and sales because a court understanding these transactions took place would be precluded under the UCC from awarding lost note status when requested. The UCC prohibits providing replacement notes to entities that have sold the notes to others, especially when the reliance is made on being a previous owner of the note but not the current owner of the note.

Lenders do not want courts to see that the notes and mortgages were sold two to three times in completely independent sales according to the pooling agreements but never recorded in the local property clerk record.

Lender hides the fact of default servicing and foreclosure operations controlled by the National Servicing Platforms, a subsidiary of which also runs the foreclosure mill lawyer operations.

What Lenders Do NOT Want the Court to See

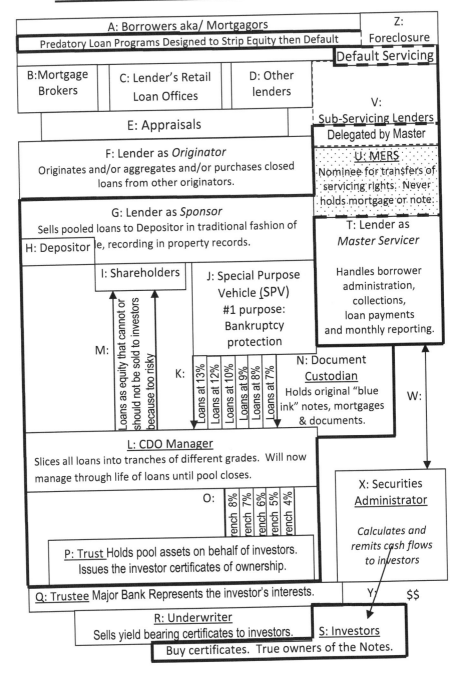

A: Borrowers aka/ Mortgagors
Predatory Loan Programs Designed to Strip Equity then Default

Z: Foreclosure

Default Servicing

B: Mortgage Brokers

C: Lender's Retail Loan Offices

D: Other lenders

V: Sub-Servicing Lenders Delegated by Master

E: Appraisals

F: Lender as *Originator*
Originates and/or aggregates and/or purchases closed loans from other originators.

U: MERS
Nominee for transfers of servicing rights. Never holds mortgage or note.

G: Lender as *Sponsor*
Sells pooled loans to Depositor in traditional fashion of [sale], recording in property records.

H: Depositor

T: Lender as *Master Servicer*
Handles borrower administration, collections, loan payments and monthly reporting.

I: Shareholders

J: Special Purpose Vehicle (SPV)
#1 purpose: Bankruptcy protection

M: Loans as equity that cannot or should not be sold to investors because too risky

K: Loans at 13% | Loans at 12% | Loans at 10% | Loans at 9% | Loans at 8% | Loans at 7%

N: Document Custodian
Holds original "blue ink" notes, mortgages & documents.

W:

L: CDO Manager
Slices all loans into tranches of different grades. Will now manage through life of loans until pool closes.

O: Tranch 8% | Tranch 7% | Tranch 6% | Tranch 5% | Tranch 4%

X: Securities Administrator
Calculates and remits cash flows to investors

P: Trust Holds pool assets on behalf of investors. Issues the investor certificates of ownership.

Q: Trustee Major Bank Represents the investor's interests.

Y: $$

R: Underwriter
Sells yield bearing certificates to investors.

S: Investors
Buy certificates. True owners of the Notes.

NRM Lender's hide their "hidden profit" area of G-H-I-J-K-L-M-N-O-P.

NRM Lenders conceal improperly recorded sales and transfers because the NRM Lender does not want to buy back the defaulted loan. For this reason, NRM Lenders conceal the properly recorded sale requirements in the pooling and servicing agreement. Violation and false attestation may subject the lender to SEC legal actions including fines and imprisonment. If the mortgage is labeled "defective" due to improper recording, the lender will be in violation of the pooling and servicing agreement and <u>be required to immediately buy back the defaulted mortgage at the original loan amount.</u> This is a standard provision in pooling and servicing agreements after a provisional period (usually 60-180 days) from the original inception date of the pool. Recording defects are very serious in pooling agreements because they cause ownership to be questionable.

Lenders do not want courts to know Document Custodians rarely lose notes, or the extensive qualifications and systems in place to track and insure the safety and access to notes as detailed in the diagram and key notes of *Document Custodian Holds the Original "Blue Ink" Signed Note.*

Lenders sheepishly pretend they lost the note, submit false affidavits to that effect and hope the parties to the foreclosure don't raise the proper document custodian issues.

Lenders rarely show proof of asking the Document Custodian for the original note because it will show the lender is *not* the current owner of record.

Many lenders simply present the original note into court as the current holder of record original, when it is not. The current holder's original will have proper transfers on it or attached as an allonge.

Lenders do not want courts to see MERS® for what it is, an electronic system of transferring loan servicing, and never a holder of the original note. The ruse of MERS® as owner of the note is still playing out in many courts, despite widespread knowledge of this sham.

Lenders do not want the court to take notice of falsely filed affidavits submitted on lost note claims stating MERS® as proper owner, and signed by an employee of the lender or servicer.

Lenders perpetuate the lost note fraud by referring to their MERS® electronic registration database of loan servicing as "the real current owner" hoping the court believes that lie. This is illegal to do in some states including Florida where the MERS® claim is forbidden both at law and by MERS® themselves.

Lenders do not want courts to see that MERS® , according to the pooling and servicing agreement and to effect the bankruptcy protection of the "hidden profit" G-H-I-J-K-L-M-N-O-P areas, may only transfer servicing *after* the Depositor (H) has received a properly transferred property clerk recorded note and mortgage.

Lenders do not want the court to see the predatory loan programs designed to lure borrowers in with super low interest "teasers", negative amortization that strips equity because the principal increases, the loan defaults and the lenders win the property in foreclosure away from the real investors.

Lenders do not want courts to see they are psychologically torturing borrowers desiring true loan modification remedies by using sophisticated passive aggressive phone methods coincidental with aggressive collection activities. Cooperating is not only a Housing and Urban Development law; it is "doing the right thing".

Modifying is a financial loser for NRM Lenders while foreclosing is a financial windfall to them. For this reason, lenders do all they can to hide their true predatory default servicing nature while they move along dual tracks to foreclosure with the borrower.

Oftentimes this "carrot" of settlement possibility disarms a borrower to rightfully protect themselves against the foreclosure action. By the time many borrowers find out the real intent behind the meaningless "go rounds" with the lender, the home has been lost to summary judgment in court.

Modification is not a voluntary lender option in most cases. The threat of investor lawsuits, the profit in foreclosure, the chaos in loss mitigation plays to foreclosure, not loan modifications. Lenders are trying to make everyone *think* a good long term loan modification solution is possible. Loan modifications produce little profit and present legal vulnerability by investors. Even though investors often desire a good modification, it conflicts with the lender's agenda.

Modifications over 5% of the number of loans in a pool may also be strictly prohibited under the pooling and servicing agreements and IRS tax rules. Tax rules have been relaxed but still have stringent guidelines. The issue is "static" pools and tax pass through benefits.

The bottom line is profit. Lenders are not satisfied to earn a few thousand dollars on a loan modification when they can earn the full amount of the home sold in foreclosure, or close to it, and dissolve the threat of investor lawsuits in the process.

The lender wants to appear as very cooperative in court. A good willed entity trying to work with an unfortunate borrower experiencing financial hardship by no fault of the lender. Instead, the predatory lender is acting quite the opposite on a fast track to foreclosure. The default servicing arms of the lender, backed by the national servicing platforms education, teach proven techniques to staff. Methods to produce anxiety, frustration eventually anger the borrower. The target of this treatment is to prompt borrowers to ignore the lender and in so doing set themselves up to lose in court via summary judgment. Passive aggressive phone abuse skills are only one tool in the aggressive default loan servicing staff's toolkit.

Lenders do not want courts to find their foreclosure lawsuits are frivolous for any or all the reasons above. Caught in that trap, Lenders will hide behind their attorneys. The attorneys are the ones who may be charged with filing frivolous lawsuits, not the lenders. Courts have rules for attorneys to follow. Attorneys operate in much the same manner as their lender clients. It is a risk reward evaluation. The risk is usually a slap on the wrist or a small fine, or some court and attorney costs in the rare case where this claim is made and substantiated.

NRM Lenders do not want the court to see or understand their Collateralized Debt Obligation and Credit Default Swap Agreements and Swap Counterparties, or Credit Default Swap enterprise that takes place in the Special Purpose Vehicle (SPV) area of the hidden profits section. Nor do they want the court to recognize that the SPV enterprise assets simply vanish once the swaps and collateralized debt obligations are sold and resold into the marketplace. Also, there are no employees or offices to pursue for explanation or to hold anyone accountable.

• **What Lenders Want the Foreclosure Court To Believe**

Lenders want the court to believe that the Borrower (A) received a good loan that they now cannot afford to pay. Lenders want to portray their Default Servicing (V) as trying to modify the loan but the borrower either isn't cooperative or does not qualify for a modification. In the case of the NRM Lender, very often nothing is farther from the truth.

Lenders want the court to believe the original mortgage and note is the current mortgage and note and will state and swear to just about anything, even if it is a blatant lie, which in many cases it is, to have this falsehood believed by the court. Lenders want the court to believe the lender is losing money because the borrower isn't paying the mortgage payment, also a lie, in many cases. The hidden profits already earned by NRM Lenders are astronomical in relation to the mortgage amount in a foreclosure case. Imagine the audacity of claiming you are losing money when in fact you have earned several times the mortgage face amount. This is just par for the course with NRM Lenders.

Lenders want the court to believe that Investors, through their Trustee, have given the right to foreclosure either to the Trustee or the lender with instructions to allow the lender to be awarded the property in foreclosure. Lenders want the court to believe they are the proper party to be awarded the property. This is usually far from the truth.

The single most relevant document to prove this fact is the Pooling and Servicing Agreement. Then the Document Custodian (N) agreements and records of the CDO Manager (L) come high up on the list. Lenders also want the court to believe the proper chain of property note transfers and recordings were followed by using MERS® as the nominee, even if it was not. An entire diagram section has been devoted in this book to the MERS® ruse in this regard, a proven sham.

What Lenders Want the Court to Believe

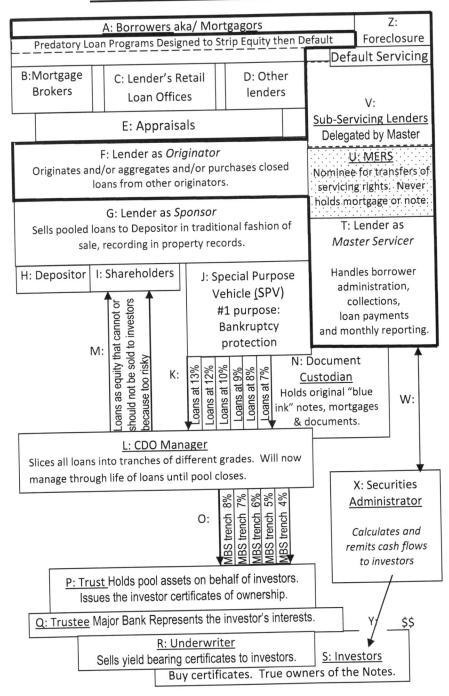

A: Borrowers aka/ Mortgagors
Predatory Loan Programs Designed to Strip Equity then Default

Z: Foreclosure

Default Servicing

B: Mortgage Brokers

C: Lender's Retail Loan Offices

D: Other lenders

V: Sub-Servicing Lenders Delegated by Master

E: Appraisals

F: Lender as *Originator*
Originates and/or aggregates and/or purchases closed loans from other originators.

U: MERS
Nominee for transfers of servicing rights. Never holds mortgage or note.

G: Lender as *Sponsor*
Sells pooled loans to Depositor in traditional fashion of sale, recording in property records.

T: Lender as *Master Servicer*

H: Depositor

I: Shareholders

J: Special Purpose Vehicle (SPV)
#1 purpose: Bankruptcy protection

Handles borrower administration, collections, loan payments and monthly reporting.

M:

Loans as equity that cannot or should not be sold to investors because too risky

K: Loans at 13% | Loans at 12% | Loans at 10% | Loans at 9% | Loans at 8% | Loans at 7%

N: Document Custodian
Holds original "blue ink" notes, mortgages & documents.

W:

L: CDO Manager
Slices all loans into tranches of different grades. Will now manage through life of loans until pool closes.

O: MBS trench 8% | MBS trench 7% | MBS trench 6% | MBS trench 5% | MBS trench 4%

X: Securities Administrator
Calculates and remits cash flows to investors

P: Trust Holds pool assets on behalf of investors. Issues the investor certificates of ownership.

Q: Trustee Major Bank Represents the investor's interests.

Y: $$

R: Underwriter
Sells yield bearing certificates to investors.

S: Investors
Buy certificates. True owners of the Notes.

Chapter 14

The Hidden National Servicing Platform Layer

- **National Servicing Platform**
- **Information Service Provider**
- **Default Solutions Provider**
- **Foreclosure Mills**
- **Default Servicing**
- **Dual Tracks To Foreclosure**

Herein lays the awesome clandestine powerhouse that provides the host of services to make the securitized mortgage backed lending and pooling operations possible. The National Servicing Platform companies are huge stock exchange giants with strong client bases and cash flow. Anyone interested can find all the information they need from published sources. The fact these giants of securitization services run mostly "in the background" is a testament to their logistically integrated achievements.

These servicing platforms perform services for a large percentage of all servicing lenders, not just non-regulated subprime lenders.

The platforms operate electronic data processing as well as operations that require personnel including default servicing and lender attorney operations. The platforms run foreclosure mills and their armies of attorneys that handle bulk foreclosures. The platforms also handle and coordinate most aspects of the lender's in-house legal operations.

The Hidden National Servicing Platform Layer

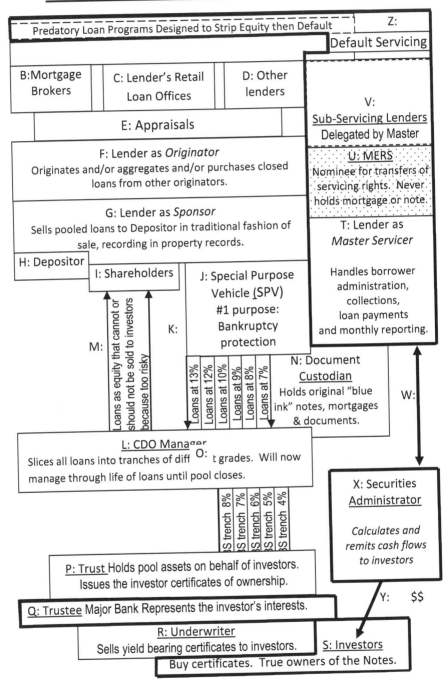

They perform default servicing and foreclosure operations for the lenders, and much more.

These operations are run strictly behind the scenes. Their reach crosses all aspects of lender, investor, and borrower operations, and everything in between, including court. This is the real power and brains of the securitized mortgage backed lending and pooling operations. These facilitators make it all possible.

NATIONAL MORTGAGE SERVICING PLATFORM: When Sponsors design their securitized transactions, they can contract with a national mortgage servicing platform. These platforms provide servicing solutions to the sponsors, the investor transaction and servicers dealing on an everyday basis with the borrowers on mortgages in the pools as well as the daily interactions with the investors… and anything in between. An example of this in the real world might be ServiceLink, "a leading provider of origination and default servicing and the national mortgage services platform for the Fidelity National Financial family of companies (NYSE:FNF)".[11] This company serves many of the biggest lenders/servicers.

INFORMATION SERVICE PROVIDER: This is a unit, division, subsidiary, etc., of the National Mortgage Servicing Platform that provides complete suites of mortgage services, such as the title, settlement, appraisal, appraisal review, asset management, servicing, default servicing and other related services for the underlying mortgages. In the real world this might be a company like Fidelity National Information Services.

DEFAULT SOLUTIONS SERVICE PROVIDER: A unit, division, subsidiary, affiliate, etc., of the Information Service Provider that provides default and foreclosure solutions for loan servicers. In the real world this might be Fidelity National Default Solutions. This company claims to handle more than half of the residential mortgage servicers in the United States. These providers can manage the

---

[11] www.servicelinkfnf.com

lender/servicer's in-house legal proceedings. They can also manage the outside third party attorneys working on the servicing lender's behalf, popularly dubbed "foreclosure mills" by those in the industry.

NOTE: The Fidelity National companies mentioned above, do not appear to have any relation with Fidelity Investment Group (fidelity.com).

FORECLOSURE MILLS: These are veritable armies of front line law firm attorneys working on behalf of default servicing lenders, but hired, managed and accountable to the Default Solutions Service Provider. Each foreclosure mill routinely files thousands of new cases a month. Different states have different mortgage foreclosure procedures. The assembly line aspect of foreclosure mills is a double edged sword. On the one hand, the sheer volume and fact a substantial amount of borrowers do not timely answer legal actions, produces a substantial number of homes won in foreclosure by summary judgment. On the other, the disorganized chaos that defines the busy foreclosure mill law firm often results in failure to act in accordance with the rules and statutes of the courts in which state the foreclosure is taking place. The rush by these attorneys to get paid, presents an opportunity for beating the foreclosure mills at their own game. While exact statistics are hard to find on the success ratio of these foreclosure mills, within the industry it's commonly thought to be very high, somewhere in the 95% success range.

DEFAULT SERVICING:
The lenders take pride in their default servicing model. It is a tough side of their business and involves a certain genius that includes using tactics that combine information that is partially true, partially false and completely false. Operations designed to hide the real identity of sponsors and sometimes even deny that sponsors exist. The sponsors, in this end of the business, differ from the sponsors on the diagram. The sponsor in this arena refers to the National Servicing Platform and their subsidiary and ancillary operations.

Loans start out in regular daily loan servicing. Billing, collecting and paying taxes, insurance and administrative duties are performed as required. If a borrower gets in trouble, the collection departments attempt to will help borrowers get current again, within their capabilities.

When the Lender as Sponsor (G) sells the mortgages to the Depositor (H) and the loans enter the hidden profit areas, the actual servicing of the loan is "peeled" off and given to the Lender as Master Servicer (T) or a qualified third party or affiliate. MERS® (U) can be used to keep track of any transfers of servicing rights and sub-servicing (V) Lenders can be designated by the Master Servicer (T). The Master Servicer rarely performs daily administrative duties with borrowers; instead they delegate this responsibility to qualified sub-servicers (V).

In exchange for performing the servicing on timely loans, servicers receive a percentage of the monthly payments collected. Servicing loans that are not in default is a straight forward business.

Default servicing on the other hand can become a down and dirty battle between the borrower and lender. It involves dunning borrowers, collections, threats, and deceitful phone games because the servicing lender does not want loan modification where they earn comparatively little money in modifying. Default servicing lenders want to foreclosure and make large windfall profits in the range of the value on a home acquired in foreclosure. Default servicers employ their own set of strong arm techniques on borrowers, one of which is the foreclosure mill attorneys.

The Master Servicing Agreements generally say that when a loan becomes delinquent the Servicer is to try their best to contact the borrower and attempt to bring the loan current. This is also in compliance with federal regulations to do the same (example HUD). If the borrower continues to be late on their payments the loan moves to different departments until it is 60 – 90 or more days late when it goes to the Loss Mitigation department or one that has similar functions under a different name.

The borrowers are then asked to provide financial worksheets that itemize all their individual income and expenses. They are asked to write a hardship letter detailing the circumstances that brought them to this point and the possibilities of coming out of it. Borrowers are asked to provide updates on their employment and to submit bank statements, pro forma financial profit and loss statements if they are self employed, and to list their available cash and assets on hand. Evaluation of this information will determine if the borrower can save their home, or will have to sell it.

Regardless, the NRM Lender exit strategy is foreclosure and the NRM Lenders have perfected the techniques of dangling the "carrot" of a good loan modification settlement while barreling down the highway to foreclosure. In many cases, the settlement process is merely designed to provide false hope and disarm the borrower until it is too late and foreclosure has been accomplished. This is called pursuing dual tracks to foreclosure.

DUAL TRACKS TO FORECLOSURE: At this point the borrower has demonstrated an ongoing intention not to bring the mortgage current. Default servicing via the Loss Mitigation Department will now begin to engage tactics to aggressively seek payment in full of the arrears or a workout that would include this.

The phone tactics used may serve to fully antagonize the borrower to the point that the borrower just stops staying in contact out of frustration. Some of these tactics include:
- Making the borrower tell the same story over and over to various persons, all of which can't help but have listened.
- Long wait times.
- An automatic disconnection after long waits forcing the process to start all over again.

Recurring same scenario procedures are often necessary due to the fact that the borrowers have to work their way up the chain of servicers. In many cases, the initial servicer is actually a sub-servicer who does not have any modification discretion. There may be several sub-servicers up to the Master Servicer (T) who makes a final decision only after consulting the Trustee (Q) representing the investors (S) in the Trust (P).

The track up to the decision makers may be a very time consuming and painful one for the borrower, sometimes taking a few months. Borrowers that try to sell their homes for example and spend extensive efforts to make a contract and send it to the lender are often exasperated by 2-3 months of decision time which inevitably kills the deal. Lenders take no responsibility for this financially and lay all the blame on the borrower. The borrower is forced to try and find another buyer and go through the same scenario. In a buyer's market, taking two to three months to accept or reject a contract offer should be criminal and subject the lender to reasonable penalties but it is not. It's just another lender tactic, accepted by the court. One reason for this may be that the judge does not understand the process. Once judges do understand, they may order responses within specified times. This is a target of the borrower's attorney to accomplish.

These are only a few of the many tactics used by lenders. While borrowers try to navigate the default servicing labyrinth, their homes are moving closer to foreclosure. Lender reps are skilled at keeping borrowers hopeful right up until the very end. Borrowers often think, and wrongfully so, that avoidance of litigation is a meaningful sign of good faith in the loan modification negotiation. This is absolutely not the case even though many loss mitigation specialists working for the lender might give borrowers that impression.

Part Three
Fighting Foreclosure

The value of credible mortgage analysis is to clearly establish where both parties stand. Coming into the foreclosure stage, the lender is going to seek Summary Judgment in court stating there are no material facts to challenge that will prevent the judgment of foreclosure being issued.

The lender will do everything in their power to avoid the process of discovery, especially credible forensic mortgage analysis inspired discovery from a firm suspecting material issues of mortgage toxicity. The NRM Lender does not want to be faced with a judge conducting their own trial based upon discovery and credible forensic loan analysis and discovery in the process.

The Lender expects to submit their side of things and have their accounting and claims be accepted and ruled upon, just like that. NRM Lender attorneys have well seasoned skills at responding to attorney allegations and borrower claims. They understand borrower attorney claims are merely allegations and evidentiary findings submitted into evidence by less than credible forensic experts can be challenged and thrown out if all the requirements of the rules of evidence are not met.

If the lender is a predatory lender or one in violation of congressionally legislated government agency regulations, they can be stopped in their tracks. Congress has empowered borrowers and their attorneys to fight predatory lenders in foreclosure. Remember, once the home is lost or sold in foreclosure, the same consumer protections do not exist. The best time to act on forensic loan compliance investigations is as soon as possible in the case.

If the loan has violations, the lender is required under the law to be dealt with in court according to specific remedies and accounting. The borrower may even have the right to roll the loan back to its original loan amount and cancel the loan, apply all payments made to principal reduction, further reduce principal by the amount of closing costs and title charges paid, receive statutory, civil and actual damages as well as attorney and court costs.

In foreclosure, the statute of limitations in terms of the borrower gaining financial claims to offset lender claims in the form of defensive recoupment is extended out for as long as the borrower owns the property.

Many predatory lenders are actually foreclosing on properties they have not properly established ownership of. Credible mortgage analysis can identify issues such as this for the court and when an expert is provided to meet the standards of evidence being allowed into court, can shift the burden of disproving the forensic analysis evidentiary findings, onto the Lender. This is a strong legal strategy.

Most lenders will not answer discovery. They would rather settle. Good settlement for a borrower who wants to keep their home means a good long term loan modification with equity in the property, a low fixed interest rate, an abandonment of all the excess charges and a payment linked to real earnings, not fictitious income. When a borrower wants to sell, good settlement is a deed-in-lieu with no summary judgment, allowing the borrower to simply walk away clean.

Turning the tide requires producing material issues in a non-objectionable form, by an expert third party, submitted into evidence and made as the basis of seeking violation remedies that empower the borrower and not the lender.

Chapter 15

Walking Away From Secured Mortgage Debt Free and Clear is NOT Realistic

Discharging primary dwelling mortgage debt is a controversial topic with different opinions on all sides. The discussion of fault is a moot point from a forensic mortgage analysts' perspective. The findings speak for themselves. If the fault is to the borrower and not to the lender, findings will indicate this.

It is disingenuous, misleading, and hurtful to tell borrowers that they can walk away free of mortgage debt when facing foreclosure due to forensic evidentiary findings or anything else. That is a very remote possibility. If a lender is court ordered to accept a borrower's tender offer and ignores it, the borrower may be able to walk away without any mortgage debt however, the likelihood is extremely low. The target should be a great loan modification.

Quiet Title
Some highly regarded attorneys in the foreclosure realm believe that borrowers who cast enough doubt on the ownership of the note will eventually be able to "quiet title" the property and receive the home for free. The problem is that quiet title is considered by some highly regarded legal minds as jurisdictionally weak, on the premise it can be challenged later on in the broader jurisdictional sense if the real owner ever shows up. This is an impediment to title which can cause problems down the road, when the borrower attempts to sell or get another mortgage on the property.

This is why title companies and lenders insist on chains of title history. In the U.S., title insurance companies issue title insurance based on the chain of title to the property when it is transferred. The abstract of title will include a brief history of claims that can be made against the property. If you can get an attorney to validate the title to the property (with an attorney's opinion of title) and the title insurance company to accept this, quiet title may work well. But it should not be considered "free and clear" ownership with a warrantable title. This is not getting a property for free in the classical sense with peace of mind and full and inalienable rights to sell the property and warrant against future challenges to ownership.

Show Me the Note
There is also a belief that the "show me the note" defense will produce a home for free. This is another gross misconception bred from a lack of in-depth knowledge of the securitized transaction. While the lender trying to foreclose may admittedly not be the appropriate party to press foreclosure on the borrower, it does not mean the borrower will get the home for free. The case can be properly brought back with the correct parties. Pooling and servicing agreements are very clear in that the mortgage is owned by the investors who purchased them. This is easily established in all securitized mortgage transactions.

The fact that those responsible to the investors did not do all they should have, and may have even sold and resold the same mortgages as well as misrepresented the credit of the borrowers, doesn't mean the investors should not be acknowledged as the rightful owners of the mortgage.

Judges understand this even though they may be confused by servicing lenders who misrepresent that they own the mortgages and attempt to acquire the property in foreclosure unscrupulously. The fact that the borrower was given a mortgage is clear. The fact the investors purchased it is also clear.

This confusion of claims to foreclose that are not made by the investors, the rightful owners, or the Trustee, is probably the reason why many judges allow foreclosures to move sideways. One hope may be that a good loan modification can be performed. From a winning against foreclosure perspective, strong discovery may provide significant offsets against amounts owed, and in a best case scenario, could prove that the investors in fact do not own that mortgage because the transfer was defective according to the pooling and servicing agreements. This was discussed at length in the diagrams section of Part Two of this book.

If ownership has not been allotted to the investors because the NRM Lender or Depositor (H) did not properly transfer the mortgage or cure a material defect within the time subscribed, then the mortgage is in limbo. It must be reimbursed to the Investors and the NRM Lender would then be in a position to foreclose on their behalf. Who wants to pay full price for a defaulted mortgage knowing they are locked into a loss? Who wants to reimburse collateralized debt obligations and credit default swaps on repeated sales of the mortgage? Too many problematic issues present themselves. Settlement is much easier. The borrower is still not going to walk away free, but in the interest of fairness, the judge may apply some profits against the lender if they can be assessed to be due using something like forensic mortgage analysis.

This way, the judge is not forced to make a potentially life altering decision (for the borrower) under ambiguous allegations and claims coming from all sides, until the facts come out in the particular case.

Rescission and Bankruptcy
Rescission, also known as loan cancellation is covered in detail in an upcoming chapter. This is the one, if not the strongest, remedy a borrower has against a predatory lender. Even so, there is a belief by some that the rescission or cancellation option of TILA and HOEPA entitles cancellation of the security interest in the debt and therefore entitles it to be included in bankruptcy as an unsecured debt. It is not realistic however to suggest to a borrower that bankruptcy judges are going to give away mortgages to borrowers for free in bankruptcy. Bankruptcy laws are not designed to let borrowers off the hook for

lawful mortgages. In fact, at this point, bankruptcy options exclude benefiting borrowers against creditors that maintain mortgages secured by the underlying property. Federal and State laws and courts are not in favor of letting borrowers walk away free from mortgages unless undisputable evidence is submitted to substantiate why this action should take place. Even the immense powers of TILA and HOEPA are not designed to let borrowers walk away from mortgage obligations free and clear.

It is important to clear the misconception of getting a home for free through discovery type of defenses, such as Show Me the Note and the host of other important issues discussed by credible sources. Just beware of blogs and misinformed media sources that do not have the credentials to be proffering opinions. Discovering toxicity and undermining the ability to foreclose does not mean getting a home for free, in any sense. It may mean living in the property or having possession of it during the foreclosure process until a determination is made by the courts, without paying mortgage payments if that is the case but this is not getting the property for free. And as mentioned, it can backfire with huge costs to the borrower.

The object is to work within the governmental agency laws to negotiate the best loan modification settlement. Whether it is to save or sell the home.

Chapter 16

TILA- RESPA-HOEPA-UDAP

TILA

The Truth in Lending Act (TILA) provides broad coverage protection on loans made to consumers. It provides violation remedies that are stipulated, rather than interpretive, meaning the financial and other remedies are specific and mandated. For refinance loans on primary dwellings made to consumers, TILA also provides rescission or cancellation of the underlying security interest as well as financial and other remedies. Violations of the HOEPA provisions of TILA, aka Section 32 High Rate, High Fees, and High Cost loans, provide a double up of financial remedies, once for TILA and then again for HOEPA.

Purpose and Coverage
The purpose of Regulation Z is to promote the informed use of consumer credit by requiring disclosures about its terms and costs. The regulation also gives consumers the right to cancel certain credit transactions that involve a lien on a consumer's principal dwelling and provides a means for fair and timely resolution of credit billing disputes. The regulation requires a maximum interest rate to be stated in variable-rate contracts secured by the consumer's dwelling. It also imposes limitations on home equity plans and high interest mortgages (Reg. Z § 226.32). The regulation prohibits certain acts or practices in connection with credit secured by a consumer's principal dwelling. (Reg. Z § 226.1(b))

Reg. Z applies to all banks, lenders, and sellers whether foreign (chartered in or having a branch in the United States), or domestic, as long as the loan was made and funded in the United States. The regulation does not apply to a foreign branch of a U.S. bank when the foreign branch extends credit to a U.S. citizen residing or visiting abroad or to a foreign national abroad. (FRB-OSC § 226.1(c) (1))

Refinancing and assumption is covered if the lender receives an application for the transaction. The TILA does not apply to loan modifications of an existing obligation's terms that do not constitute a refinance loan. (FRB-OSC § 226.1(d)(5)(1)(i)).

TILA requires creditors to make disclosures clearly and conspicuously in writing, in a form that the consumer may keep. U.S.C. § 226.5(a)(1); U.S.C. § 1632(a).

Codification, Authorities and Legal Sources

Federal Reserve Board's (FRB) Truth in Lending Official Staff Commentary (FRB-OSC) To Regulation Z.
Codification: Official Staff Commentary to Regulation Z codified to 12 C.F.R. Part § 226.
Authority: 12 USC § 3806, 15 USC § 1604 and § 1637(c)(5).

Official staff interpretations of the regulation are published in a commentary that is normally updated annually in March. Good faith compliance with the commentary protects creditors from civil liability under the act. In addition, the commentary includes mandates, which are not necessarily explicit in Regulation Z, on disclosures or other actions required of creditors. In order to comply with the Regulation Z, it is critical to reference and rely on the commentary. (Truth in Lending, Comptroller's Handbook, October 2008).

FRB Commentary is Dispositive: The Federal Reserve Board's Official Staff Commentary on Regulation Z is dispositive. (U.S. Supreme Court case Ford Motor Credit v. Milhollin (aka Millhollin) [here mentioned in pertinent part:] "Unless demonstrably irrational,

Federal Reserve Board staff opinions construing the Act or Regulation should be dispositive for several reasons. [444 U.S. 555, 566]"

Truth in Lending Act (Regulation Z)
FDIC Law, Regulations, Related Acts
Codification: Regulation Z codified to 12 C.F.R. Part § 226.
Authority: 12 USC § 3806; 15 USC § 1604 and § 1637(c)(5) and § 1639(1).

Regulation Z is issued by the Board of Governors of the Federal Reserve System to implement the federal Truth in Lending Act, which is contained in title I of the Consumer Credit Protection Act, as amended (15 USC § 1601 *et seq.*).

Governing Agencies:
- Office of the Comptroller of the Currency, Treasury (OCC)
- Board of Governors of the Federal Reserve System (FRB, Board)
- Federal Deposit Insurance Corporation (FDIC)
- Office of Thrift Supervision, Treasury (OTS)
- National Credit Union Administration (NCUA)

TILA Federal violation remedies fall into a few distinct areas including:
- reimbursement of all closing costs and fees paid on the loan. Cases of additional HOEPA violations can result in TWICE the amounts
- rescission (apply all the interest to principle amounts and cancel the loan)
- statutory damages up to $2,000 per combined loan exposure
- civil damages up to $500,000 in a class action
- reimbursement of attorneys fees, etc.

The documentation aspect: TILA requires specific disclosures before the closing of a credit transaction.

Disclosures must be made "clearly and conspicuously in writing, in a form that the consumer may keep" § 1632(a); § 226.17(a)(1); and in the case of Home Equity Loans "shall be grouped together and segregated from all unrelated information". § 226.5(b)(1); A lawsuit for violation of TILA may be based upon a lenders failure to comply with disclosure requirements. U.S.C. §§ 1631-34.

Disclosures, for example, under The Act must meet certain

- form of disclosures and computation of finance charges and Annual Percentage Rate (APR)
- conspicuous format
- timing of the disclosures
- description of legal obligations of the parties
- estimates disclosed when information necessary to accurate disclosure is unknown at the time
- content of disclosures
- meeting of requirements of the Act
- finance charge computations
- annual percentage rate APR computations
- additional specifications and regulations.

TILA requires clear, accurate and conspicuous disclosure of loan terms. A critical aspect of TILA is the right to rescind (cancel) notice required. Two copies of the 3-day right to rescind (cancel) notice must be given to EACH borrower who has an ownership interest in the property (§ 226.15(b)). When more than one borrower has the right to rescind, the exercise of the right by one borrower shall be effective as to all borrowers. (§ 226.15(a)(4)). The notice must meet all the requirements clearly and conspicuously (§ 226.15(b)) including how to exercise the right (§ 226.15(b)(3), the effects of rescission(§ 226.15(b)(4) and the date the rescission period ends(§ 226.15(b)(5).

Finance Charges and APR (Annual Percentage Rate) aspect:

Most TILA violations involve the creditor's failure to charge the correct amount, failure to disclose all the material terms, or failure to provide necessary forms or documents required by the Truth in Lending Act, that conspicuously disclose transaction details such as:

- charges by third parties
- mortgage broker fees
- <u>Inclusion</u> of the following types of charges:
  1. Interest, time price differential, and any amount payable under an add-on or discount system of additional charges.
  2. Service, transaction, activity, and carrying charges, including any charge imposed on a checking or other transaction account to the extent that the charge exceeds the charge for a similar account without a credit feature.
  3. Points, loan fees, assumption fees, finder's fees, and similar charges.
  4. Appraisal, investigation, and credit report fees.
  5. Premiums or other charges for any guarantee or insurance protecting the creditor against the consumer's default or other credit loss.
  6. Charges imposed on a creditor by another person for purchasing or accepting a consumer's obligation, if the consumer is required to pay the charges in cash, as an addition to the obligation, or as a deduction from the proceeds of the obligation.
  7. Premiums or other charges for credit life, accident, health, or loss-of-income insurance, written in connection with a credit transaction.
  8. Premiums or other charges for insurance against loss of or damage to property, or against liability arising out of the ownership or use of property, written in connection with a credit transaction.
  9. Discounts for the purpose of inducing payment by a means other than the use of credit.
  10. Debt cancellation fees. Charges or premiums paid for debt cancellation coverage written in connection with a credit

165

transaction, whether or not the debt cancellation coverage is insurance under applicable law.

- <u>Exclusion</u> of the following types of charges:
    1. Application fees
    2. Charges for actual unanticipated late payment
    3. Charges for paying items that overdraw an account
    4. Fees charged for participation in a credit plan
    5. Seller's points
    6. Interest forfeited as a result of an interest reduction
    7. Real-estate related fees. I.e.: Fees for title examination, abstract of title, title insurance, property survey, and similar purposes. Fees for preparing loan-related documents, such as deeds, mortgages, and re-conveyance or settlement documents. Notary, and credit report fees. Property appraisal fees or fees for inspections to assess the value or condition of the property if the service is performed prior to closing, including fees related to pest infestation or flood hazard determinations. Amounts required to be paid into escrow or trustee accounts if the amounts would not otherwise be included in the finance charge.
    8. Discounts offered to induce payment for a purchase
    9. Premiums for insurance against loss of or damage to property
    10. Voluntary debt cancellation fees.
    11. Certain security interest charges
    12. Taxes and fees prescribed by law
    13. Taxes on security instruments
    14. Prohibited offsets
    15. and more...

In addition, Adjustable Rate Mortgages, "ARMs" must meet substantially more stringent requirements than Closed End Mortgages. For example: *Reg. Z §226.18(f) Variable rate. (1) If the annual percentage rate may increase after consummation in a transaction not secured by the consumer's principal dwelling or in a transaction secured by the consumer's principal dwelling with a term of one year or less, the following disclosures:*

166

(i) The circumstances under which the rate may increase.
(ii) Any limitations on the increase
(iii) The effect of an increase.
(iv) An example of the payment terms that would result from an increase.

Under TILA, the remedies, enforcement and liabilities are clearly delineated. Only the creditors (the ones giving the loans) are subject to civil penalties. Failing to properly, conspicuously and accurately disclose according to the act, entitles borrowers to a) damages (statutory up to $2,000 in a real estate loan; and actual damages); b) actual closing costs and fees; c) right of rescission and; d) attorney's fees.

- Statutory Damages: Violations of the general and rescission requirements to statutory damage claims (U.S.C. § 1640 Civil liability (a) Individual or class action for damages; amount of award; factors determining amount of award).Open-end mortgage transactions are awarded in an amount equal to 2x the amount of the finance charges [12]. Closed-end primary residence mortgage transactions [13] receive ONE statutory recovery of a minimum of $200 and a maximum of $2,000 for all combined disclosure violations in a particular transaction.
    - Failure of the lender to respond may result in an additional violation award of statutory damages. [14]

- Actual Damages: Consumers may receive an award in an amount equal to "any actual damage sustained by such person as a result of

---

[12] U.S.C. § 1640 (a)(2)(A)(i) in the case of an individual action twice the amount of any finance charge in connection with the transaction

[13] U.S.C. § 1640 (a)(2)(A) (iii) in the case of an individual action relating to a credit transaction not under an open end credit plan that is secured by real property or a dwelling, not less than $200 or greater than $2,000; or

[14] FDIC 6500 §130(a)(2)(A)(iii) Civil Damages: "in the case of an individual action relating to a credit transaction not under an open end credit plan that is secured by real property or a dwelling, not less than $400 or greater than $4,000"

the failure[15]" and courts may order borrowers to show how relying on the accuracy of the disclosures caused the damages claimed. In other words, borrowers may be required to show that they would have obtained a loan under better terms if they understood the disclosures if for example, the disclosures were clear and conspicuous.

RESPA

The Real Estate Settlement Procedures Act (RESPA) is a federal consumer protection law implemented and overseen by the U.S. Department of Housing and Urban Development (HUD). RESPA is designed to ensure that home buyers can make informed choices about their choice of settlement providers and that the fees they are charged in connection with the settlement process are fair and reasonable under the law.

Currently (See source data below) RESPA does not include authority for regulators to enforce important sections of the statute; there are no remedies for violations of the requirements relating to the Good Faith Estimate, Settlement Costs Booklet, or HUD-1 Settlement Statement. [16] HUD is working on changing that.

---

[15] U.S.C. § 1640 (a)(1)

[16] Source: http://www.hud.gov/offices/cir/test080522a.cfm.

HUD Written Statement of Ivy Jackson Director, Office of RESPA and Interstate Land Sales U.S. Department of Housing and Urban Development Hearing before the Committee on Small Business United States House of Representatives "Proposed Rule to Simplify and Improve the Process of Obtaining Mortgages and Reduce Consumer Settlement Costs" May 22, 2008;

"HUD, therefore, would like to work with Congress to enact legislative changes to RESPA that include:

Requiring delivery of the HUD–1 to the borrower 3 days prior to closing. Authority for the Secretary to impose civil money penalties for violations of specific RESPA

Two important violation remedies exist in the areas of specific interest to borrower's facing foreclosure: Kickbacks (12 U.S.C. § 2607(d) Penalties for Violations) and Mortgage Servicing Transfer Disclosures (24 CFR 3500.21). RESPA also provides penalties for Escrow Account violations.

TILA and HOEPA protect *"consumers in the mortgage market from unfair, abusive, or deceptive lending and servicing practices while preserving responsible lending and sustainable homeownership[17]"*. "[M]isleading disclosure is as much a violation of TILA as a failure to disclose at all". [18]. Consumers do not have the burden of showing they were misled or deceived by unclear credit terms in order to prevail. Lenders are required to comply strictly with ALL the TILA rules, not merely "attempt" to comply[19].

While proving a claim under RESPA may be difficult, using the TILA and HOEPA disclosures with RESPA required disclosure guidance is the perfect complimentary strategy. In other words, there may be no penalties for not issuing a HUD 1 Settlement Statement or Good Faith Estimate under RESPA but under TILA and HOEPA the action of not supplying these disclosures, because they are required under RESPA, can be used as the basis of a "material disclosure" violation claim. As such, when required material disclosures are not clearly and conspicuously supplied, the violation remedies can be very potent (see TILA, HOEPA in this chapter). This aspect of RESPA defined material disclosures is an important practical reason that Lender Compliance Analysis services include RESPA disclosure violations

---

sections, including sections 4 (provision of uniform settlement statement), 5 (GFE and special information (settlement costs) booklet), 6 (servicing), 8 (prohibition against kickbacks, referral fees, and unearned fees), 9 (title insurance), and portions of 10 (escrow accounts); as well as authority for the Secretary and State regulators to seek injunctive and equitable relief for violations of RESPA."

[17] Federal Reserve Board Official Staff Commentary – Final Ruling 2008 Pg 1 Pgh 1
[18] Smith v. Chapman, 614 F.2d 968,977 (5th Cir. 1980)
[19] Noel v. Fleet Finance, Inc., 971 F. Supp. 1102 (E.D. Mich. 1997).

that do not themselves have specific remedies under RESPA, but are very powerful when used with TILA and HOEPA.

To make direct RESPA violation remedies stick, RESPA examinations must show evidence of the charges being intentional. Proving "intention" in some violations may be difficult without hard evidence. For example, proving a broker or lender paid illegal cash finder's fees outside of closing is easier said than done without hard evidence.

Kickback violations, while hard to prove unless the borrower has evidence, carry a substantial penalty in the form of three times (3x) the charge. This can be meaningful, depending on the charge. For example, let's say an analysis discovers that an appraisal charge of $2,500 would normally have cost $500. This would point to a $2,000 kickback. This can result in a $6,000 (3x) civil lender liability, plus attorney's fees and court costs and the possibility of a criminal liability in the form of a $10,000 fine and imprisonment up to a year.

Kickbacks See: 12 U.S.C. § 2607(d) Penalties for Violations): Civil and criminal liability is provided for violating the prohibition against kickbacks and unearned fees, including:

- Civil liability to the parties affected, equal to (3 x) three times the amount of the referral fee, kickback, or unearned fee.
- The possibility that the costs associated with any court proceeding and reasonable attorney's fees could be recovered.
- A fine of no more than $10,000 or imprisonment for no more than 1 year or both, for each violation.

Mortgage Servicing Transfer Disclosure violations (24 CFR 3500.21) will result in actual damages, attorneys fees, and additional damages (in the case of a pattern or practice of noncompliance), as the court allows, up to $1,000. A one thousand dollar penalty may not seem like much in the scheme of a mortgage facing foreclosure with a mountain of related penalty charges and unpaid payments. The real power of this violation remedy is in the plausible threat to a lender of a class action. Although the benefit to an individual borrower is only up to $1,000 for each member of the class, the total amount of damages to a lender will be the lesser of $500,000 or 1 percent of the net worth of the lender. The threat of losing half a million dollars or one percent of the entire company's net worth, plus legal fees and court costs is a remedy that will get any lender's attention, especially considering the disclosure referenced to be supplied is a simple one page document.

In this way, RESPA may be employed by a savvy attorney to make a particularly difficult lender understand the depth of financial risk in not settling with a borrower whose attorney is capable of joining a class action. After all, class actions are often won or settled with substantial awards of legal fees added to settlement amounts.

RESPA regulates two main areas of the settlement process. These are Disclosures and Unlawful Practices by real estate settlement providers that can serve to drive up settlement costs for home buyers.

RESPA covers transactions involving a federally related mortgage loan, which includes most loans secured by a lien (first or subordinate position) on residential property. This includes: home purchase loans, refinances, lender approved assumptions, property improvement loans, equity lines of credit and reverse mortgages. Most conventional loans as well as FHA, VA and other government sponsored loan programs are included. 12 U.S.C. § 2601(1)

RESPA does not cover the following transactions: an all cash sale, a sale where the individual home seller takes back the mortgage, a rental property transaction or other business purpose transaction.

Statute of Limitations: Unlimited as a defense to foreclosure in the nature of a set off or recoupment. One year for affirmative claims of kickbacks and/or fee-sharing. 12 U.S.C. § 2614

HOEPA

The Home Ownership and Equity Protection Act of 1994, known as HOEPA, is an amendment to the Truth in Lending Act (TILA). It was enacted by Congress in response to substantive abuses by creditors offering alternative high interest rate home loans to residents of certain geographic areas. The statute was enacted to ensure that these consumers would be able to obtain credit in an unimpeded flow under a safety net of protections against abusive practices.

HOEPA refers to credit transactions and specifically this case, mortgages secured by primary dwellings other than a purchase money mortgage, a reverse mortgage transaction, or an open-end loan. HOEPA addresses certain deceptive and unfair practices in what are known as High Rate, High Fee loans. These are sometimes referred under the section of Regulation Z which implements the Truth in Lending Act (TILA) and referred to as "Section 32 Mortgages".

If a loan is included in the coverage and qualifies for HOEPA, the benefits for violations can substantially increase the financial offsets and setoffs in the nature of a defensive recoupment provided under TILA in addition to the possibility of rescission benefits.

The rules primarily affect refinancing and home equity installment loans that also meet the definition of a high-rate or high-fee loan. The rules do *not* cover loans to buy or build a home, reverse mortgages, or home equity lines of credit (similar to revolving credit accounts).

HOEPA allows the borrower to deduct any finance charge that was paid including pre-paid finance charges to the Lender. The borrower will deduct only those paid to the lender. The borrower still deducts all the mortgage payments made. So the difference in the TILA calculation and the HOEPA calculation is usually relatively minor. For example, in TILA, all the finance charges permitted to be included can be deducted. If this was $7,500, these might include some charges that did not go to the lender but instead were paid by the lender to third parties, such as an appraisal and survey. In this case, for purposes of HOEPA, the $7,500 might actually turn out to be $5,000; but the rest of the additional deduction that HOEPA adds in addition to the TILA adjustments will generally mimic the TILA deductions.

Therefore, by way of example, if the TILA deductions to a $250,000 loan were $80,000 the qualifying HOEPA deductions would be an additional $77,500 in this example, reflecting the $2,500 adjustment previously mentioned. In total that would produce an adjusted loan amount required to pay off on a loan with these violations of $92,500. The loan was $250,000 not including added penalties, and the adjusted outstanding loan amount the borrower will need to refinance or come up with to cancel the loan and make a "tender offer" for the loan will now be $92,500. That is a powerful mandatory adjustment at law.

HOEPA violations give rise to "enhanced" monetary damages under (15 U.S.C. § 1640(a)(4)), namely, all payments made by the borrower. *In re Williams*, 291 B.R. 636, 663-64 (Bankr. E.D. Pa. 2003).

As with any TILA violation (see TILA section above), the extended three year right of rescission remedy runs against any assignee of the loan. (15 U.S.C. § 1641(c)). Lender's trying to avoid penalties by selling the servicing rights simply transfer the exposure to an additional lender. Lender's who are not careful to check for HOEPA violations may be inheriting toxic mortgage obligations that expose them to great financial risk. This is a reason for lenders to also use credible mortgage analysis services. An analysis is a small price to pay as TILA and HOEPA violations can expose the lender to tens of thousands of dollars in claims.

In addition, assignees "shall be subject to all claims and defenses with respect to that mortgage that the consumer could assert against the creditor." (15 U.S.C. § 1641(d)(1)). This provision reflects the FTC "Holder Rule" inasmuch as it creates assignee liability under all state and federal claims and defenses. For monetary damage claims under TILA, HOEPA provides an exception to general rule that violations must appear on the face of the documents. For this reason examinations look into the transaction, not just what is printed.

Triggers of Coverage:

There are two triggers for HOEPA coverage:

The Treasury Rate Spread: The annual percentage rate at consummation of the transaction will exceed by more than 10 percentage points on a second position mortgage, and by more than 8 percentage points on a first position mortgages closing on or after 10/01/2002; the yield on Treasury securities having comparable periods of maturity to the loan maturity as of the 15th day of the month immediately preceding the month in which the application for the extension of credit is received by the creditor; Reg. Z § 226.32(a)(1)(i).

OR:

Points and Fees: The total points and fees payable by the consumer at or before loan closing will exceed the greater of 8% of the total loan amount or $400 (adjusted annually by the Board of Governors of the Federal Reserve System ("FRB") on January 1 by the annual percentage change in the Consumer Price Index that was reported on June 1 of the preceding year), which is covered by HOEPA, pursuant to Section 129 of TILA, 15 U.S.C. § 1639, and Regulation Z, 12 C.F.R. § 226.32(a)(1)(ii).

Points and Fees include:

- All prepaid finance charges. 12 C.F.R. 226.32(b)(1)(i);
- All compensation paid to mortgage brokers. 12 C.F.R. 226.32(b)(1)(ii);
- All items paid to the lender or to a lender affiliate. 12 C.F.R. 226.32(b)(1)(iii);

Unfair, Deceptive Acts and Practices (UDAP) as reflected in all 50 States, including D.C. and Puerto Rico's consumer protection laws.

It is critical to reference the particular state the property is located in. Each state has its own consumer protection laws but they are by no means uniform. Not all UDAP regulations on the Federal level are adopted into the TILA. The basis for uniform adaptations of UDAP on the federal level might likely be the Federal Trade Commission (FTC)

Act § 45 which also serves as a model in varying degrees for State laws.

Unfair or deceptive acts or practices are a violation of Section 5(a) of the FTC Act, 15 U.S.C. § 45(a), as amended. The FTC has, can, and will bring lawsuits against lenders committing violations against borrowers, especially where the FTC desires a particular lender to cease and desist, as well as pay penalties to borrowers, disgorge profits, pay fines and be monitored in the future. The likelihood of a borrower persuading the FTC to bring an individual case is slim to none.

The importance of the FTC Act § 45 to a particular borrower is the Commission's enforcement policy against deceptive acts or practices in the mortgage related industry as it relates to particular unfair or deceptive acts or practices. The FTC has brought complaints and cases using the Federal Reserve Boards' ("FRB") Truth in Lending Act ("TILA"), Regulation Z ("Reg. Z") and Home Ownership and Equity Protection Act ("HOEPA") rules and guidance. All of these serve States in varying degrees in determining their own consumer protection UDAP laws.

According to the Federal Reserve Board's guidance, which implements TILA, TILA protects *consumers in the mortgage market from unfair, abusive, or deceptive lending and servicing practices while preserving responsible lending and sustainable homeownership*[20]*"*. There are District Court of Appeals cases affirming TILA's remedial nature and requirement of strict adherence to its provisions. "Misleading disclosure is as much a violation of TILA as a failure to disclose at all"[21]. Consumers do not have the burden of showing they were misled or deceived by unclear credit terms in order to prevail. Lenders are required to comply strictly with ALL the TILA rules, not merely "attempt" to comply[22].

---

[20] Federal Reserve Board Official Staff Commentary – Final Ruling 2008 Pg 1 Pgh 1
[21] Smith v. Chapman, 614 F.2d 968,977 (5th Cir. 1980)
[22] Noel v. Fleet Finance, Inc., 971 F. Supp. 1102 (E.D. Mich. 1997).

When an attorney is forming their pleadings on the TILA and HOEPA fronts, the FTC Section §45 cases brought and won using the UDAP aspects of the Act contain a wealth of pertinent pleadings that specifically apply to unfair or deceptive acts or practices or misleading disclosures.

On the Federal level violation remedies include extended right of rescission to three years, voiding the underlying mortgage security interest, returning all finance charges paid by the borrower including interest and closing costs, attorney fees, court costs and all other remedies under TILA and HOEPA. States are free to exceed Federal regulatory guidelines but cannot reduce them.

FTC Act § 45

Language in the very beginning of Section 45 sets out the purpose and coverage. In pertinent part: *Unfair methods of competition in or affecting commerce, and unfair or deceptive acts or practices in or affecting commerce, are hereby declared unlawful. The Commission is hereby empowered and directed to prevent unfair or deceptive acts or practices in or affecting commerce and consumers.*

"Certain elements undergird all deception cases. First, there must be a representation, omission or practice that is likely to mislead the consumer."

On the Federal level, practices that have been found misleading or deceptive in specific cases include false oral or written representations, misleading price claims, sales of services without adequate disclosures, failure to disclose information, use of bait and switch techniques and failure to perform promised services, among others. The resultant findings of deceptive acts or practices can produce substantial violation remedies in the form of civil penalty of not more than $10,000 for each violation. Individual States have varying degrees of violations and remedies.

On the Federal level, UDAP can include such concerns as:

Failure to make full, accurate, timely disclosures required under TILA, RESPA and HOEPA or engaging in prohibited practices. For example:

- the annual percentage rate (APR), in violation of Section 129(a)(2) of TILA, 15 U.S.C. § 1639(a)(2), and Section 226.32(c)(2) of Regulation Z, 12 C.F.R. § 226.32(c)(2);, regular payment amount,

- the regular payment amount, in violation of Section 129(a)(2) of TILA, 15 U.S.C. § 1639(a)(2), and Section 226.32(c)(3) of Regulation Z, 12 C.F.R. § 226.32(c)(3);

- specified variable rate information, in violation of Section 129(a)(2) of TILA, 15 U.S.C. § 1639(a)(2), and Section 226.32(c)(4) of Regulation Z, 12 C.F.R. § 226.32(c)(4);

- failing to make the disclosures described in Paragraph 18(a) and (b) above clearly and conspicuously in writing at least three business days prior to consummation of a HOEPA mortgage loan transaction, in violation of Section 129(b)(1) of TILA, 15 U.S.C. § 1639(b)(1), and Section 226.31(b) and (c)(1) of Regulation Z, 12 C.F.R. § 226.31(b) and (c)(1).

- including a prohibited "balloon payment" provision, in violation of Section 129(e) of TILA, 15 U.S.C. § 1639(e), and Section 226.32(d)(1) of Regulation Z, 12 C.F.R. § 226.32(d)(1);

- including a prohibited "increased interest rate" provision, in violation of Section 129(d) of TILA, 15 U.S.C. § 1639(d), and Section 226.32(d)(4) of Regulation Z, 12 C.F.R. § 226.32(d)(4).

- including prohibited loan terms in HOEPA mortgage loan transactions in violation of Section 45(a) of the FTC Act, 15 U.S.C. § 45(a).

- By asset based lending: by engaging in a pattern or practice of extending such credit to a consumer based on the consumer's collateral rather than considering the consumer's current and expected income, current obligations, and employment status to determine whether the consumer is able to make the scheduled payments to repay the obligation, in violation of Section 129(h) of TILA, 15 U.S.C. § 1639(h), and Section 226.32(e)(1) of Regulation Z, 12 C.F.R. § 226.32(e)(1).

- Failure to Furnish Assignee Notice.

- Spurious Open-End Credit by falsely representing to consumers that the credit offered and extended by defendants is open-end credit, as set forth in Paragraphs 26 and 27 above, defendants have engaged, and continue to engage, in deceptive acts or practices in violation of Section 5(a) of the FTC Act, 15 U.S.C. § 45(a).

Federal courts have power to grant relief pursuant to Section 13(b) of the FTC Act, 15 U.S.C. § 53(b), Section 108(c) of TILA, 15 U.S.C. § 1607(c), and their own inherent equitable powers. Individual States grant their State courts with a varying degree of remedies pursuant to the pertinent state laws.

Awards for relief are made as the Court deems necessary to prevent unjust enrichment and to redress consumer injury resulting from lender's violations of HOEPA, TILA, Regulation Z, and/or Section 5(a) of the FTC Act including, but not limited to, rescission or reformation of contracts, refund of monies paid, and/or disgorgement of ill-gotten gains; and civil damages, attorney and court costs.

Chapter 17

What is Rescission?

TILA provides an extended right of rescission (cancellation) on refinance loans on primary residences within three years of issuance when the use is personal. TILA includes home equity lines of credit. HOEPA, a section of TILA addressing high interest, high fee loans restricts the rescission to refinance loans or fixed rate second mortgages but includes additional measures and restrictions including certain triggers of coverage. Violation of TILA provides one set of financial remedies and violation of HOEPA adds additional financial remedies. Rescission and the financial offsets as a defensive recoupment can be assessed as the most significant violation and remedy provided by governmental agency regulations.

When the transaction is rescinded, all parties must be returned to their pre-transaction position and the transaction is cancelled, and significant financial remedies are applied according to the Acts.

This topic will be handled in three sections,
1. Overview.
2. Key Points.
3. The Rescission Process Must Be Followed Without Fail. This will include the Tender Offer process.

What is Rescission?

Section One:
<u>Overview</u>

Extended Rights of Rescission are considered the most powerful remedy for TILA violations. It is therefore very important to understand the following issues:

1. <u>Factors that impart The Right To Rescind:</u> Failure to deliver a materially proper disclosure notice of the right to rescind (cancel) automatically triggers an extension of the right to rescind from three (3) <u>days</u> (§ 226.23(a)(3) to three (3) <u>years</u> after consummation of the loan closing.

2. <u>Critical Procedures The Borrower Must Follow:</u>
   a) The rescission notice MUST be sent within three (3) years[23] of the loan closing. There are NO EXCEPTIONS to this rule.

   b) The rescission notice letter should be sent to:
      a. the original creditor named on the original 3-day right to rescind (cancel) notice; <u>and</u>
      b. to the current lender servicing of the loan[24]; and
      c. at the borrower's option, but highly recommended: to the "Lender's Attorney".

---

[23] Reg. Z §226.23(a)(3); FDIC 6500 § 125(f) (1) in pertinent part "within three years after the date of consummation of the transaction"

[24] FDIC 6500 § 131(d)(1) In pertinent part: "IN GENERAL.--Any person who purchases or is otherwise assigned a mortgage referred to in section 103(aa) shall be subject to all claims and defenses with respect to that mortgage that the consumer could assert against the creditor of the mortgage, unless the purchaser or assignee demonstrates, by a preponderance of the evidence, that a reasonable person exercising ordinary due diligence, could not determine, based on the documentation required by this title, the itemization of the amount financed, and other disclosure of disbursements"

c) The rescission notice may be sent by "mail, telegram, or other means of written communication[25]".

3. <u>Process Required To Effect Rescission:</u> From the moment a borrower intends to rescind the mortgage, they should begin setting up the financing they <u>must</u> have in place to pay the "tender" amount to the creditor within a short time of their accepting the tender offer. There are "necessary actions" that must be taken (to follow). It is important to mention that the borrower gets a <u>reduction</u> in the amount owed; they do <u>not</u> get the property for free. See calculating the tender amount in item 4 below the Necessary Actions.

- <u>Necessary Action 1:</u> "When a consumer rescinds a transaction, the security interest giving rise to the right of rescission becomes void and the consumer shall <u>not</u> be liable for any amount, including any finance charge[26]."

- <u>Necessary Action 2:</u> "Within 20 calendar days after receipt of a notice of rescission, the creditor shall return any money or property that has been given to anyone in connection with the transaction and shall take any action necessary to reflect the termination of the security interest." [27] The borrower may retain possession until this happens.

- <u>Necessary Action 3:</u> Creditors may not do this automatically and the borrower may decide to bring an action in court to affirm the rescission. Either way, when the "creditor has complied", "the consumer shall tender the money or property to the creditor", "the creditor's designated place of business"

---

[25] Reg. Z § 226.15 (a)(2) "To exercise the right to rescind, the consumer shall notify the creditor of the rescission by mail, telegram, or other means of written communication. Notice is considered given when mailed, or when filed for telegraphic transmission, or, if sent by other means, when delivered to the creditor's designated place of business. "

[26] Reg. Z § 226.23 (d)(1)

[27] Reg. Z § 226.23 (d)(2); Reg. Z § 226.23 (d)(2)

and this process may be "modified by court order"[28].

4. The "Tender Offer" and How It May Be Calculated[29]:
   Principal loan amount <u>minus:</u>
   - All loan payments made.
   - All loan expenses (closing costs and fees) paid according to an itemized list provided with the tender offer.
   - Any statutory civil penalties for violation of TILA.

5. <u>Special Rules That Relate to Foreclosure</u>: Courts have held[30] the three (3) year limit to rights of rescission becomes <u>unlimited</u> in time when a qualifying property is in foreclosure and the calculations to tender are intended to be used as an adjustment to a settlement amount in the form of recoupment or setoff.

6. <u>Additional rights a borrower has when their loan falls under the high interest and fee protection of HOEPA</u> (The Home Equity and Protection Act). In addition to the TILA Rescission remedies,

---

[28] Reg. Z § 226.23 (d)(3); Reg. Z § 226.23 (d)(4)
[29] Consistent with the formula used by the Ninth Circuit in <u>Semar v. Platte Valley Fed. Sav. & Loan Ass'n</u>, <u>See Semar</u> at 703 –704
[30] according to Reg. Z § 226.23 (h)(1-2 et. Seq.) [Codified to 12 C.F.R. § 226.23] (h) Special rules for foreclosures.--(1) Right to rescind. After the initiation of foreclosure on the consumer's principal dwelling that secures the credit obligation, the consumer shall have the right to rescind the transaction if: (i) A mortgage broker fee that should have been included in the finance charge was not included; or (ii) The creditor did not provide the properly completed appropriate model form in appendix H of this part, or a substantially similar notice of rescission. (2) Tolerance for disclosures. After the initiation of foreclosure on the consumer's principal dwelling that secures the credit obligation, the finance charge and other disclosures affected by the finance charge (such as the amount financed and the annual percentage rate) shall be considered accurate for purposes of this section if the disclosed finance charge:
(i) is understated by no more than $35; or
(ii) is greater than the amount required to be disclosed.

enforcement and liabilities mentioned above, HOEPA (Home Ownership and Equity Protection Act) violations entitle the qualifying borrower to deduct HOEPA damages in addition to the TILA Rescission remedies, enforcement and liabilities. These "enhanced" HOEPA damages essentially result in "double dipping". First calculate for TILA and then calculate AGAIN for HOEPA.

What is Rescission?

Section Two:
<u>Key Points</u>

In this section following Key Points will be covered:

- Statute of Limitations
- To Determine Whether the Rule Applies – Ask 3 Questions
- What Kind of Loan is Rescindable?
- Statute of Limitations
- Types of Non-rescindable Loans
- Cash-out Refinance Rules
- Structure must be borrower's Principal Dwelling
- Who is able to Rescind a Loan?
- Special Rules for Foreclosures
- Right of Rescission Requirements for Lenders
- What are the Material Disclosures?
- TILA Disclosures Must Be Accurate
- Finance Charge Accuracy
- Annual Percentage Rate – APR Accuracy
- A Word about HOEPA Loans
- Rescission Process - Notifying the Lender
- Relationship between Servicer and Creditor
- Effects of Rescission
- Assignee Liability

Statute of Limitations
- Extended right of rescission must be exercised within 3 years of the loan closing.
- No limit to offsets or setoffs in foreclosure.

To Determine Whether the Rule Applies – Ask Three Questions
- First, does Regulation Z apply to the transaction?
- Second, is the loan secured by a borrower's "principal dwelling?"
- Third, is the loan used to purchase the dwelling?

What Kind of Loan is Rescindable?
The Right of Rescission applies to non-purchase money, Regulation Z loans in which a security interest is taken in a borrower's principal dwelling. For example:
- Home equity line of credit
- An installment loan where the borrower pays a fixed amount and repays the debt on an agreed payment schedule
- A security interest that is acquired by a contractor who is also extending credit in the transaction

Types of Non-rescindable Loans
- A loan to purchase or build the borrower's principal dwelling (i.e., a residential mortgage transaction).
- A consolidation or Refinance with the same lender who already holds the mortgage and no additional funds are borrowed.
- A business-purpose loan, even though the loan is secured by the borrower's principal dwelling.
- A transaction in which a state agency is a creditor.
- A mechanic's lien where the contractor is not a party to the credit transaction.

Cash-out Refinance Rules
- The consumer is Refinancing more than they owe on their current mortgage and taking the difference out in cash.

- For a cash-out Refinancing with the same lender, only the cash-out portion is subject to the right of rescission.
- For a cash-out Refinancing with a different lender, the entire loan amount can be rescinded.

Structure must be borrower's Principal Dwelling
- A consumer can only have one principal dwelling at a time.
- A vacation or other second home would not be a principal dwelling.
- A transaction secured by a second home that is not currently being used as the borrower's principal dwelling is not rescindable, even if the consumer intends to reside there in the future.
- When a consumer buys or builds a new dwelling that will become the borrower's principal dwelling within one year, it is considered the principal dwelling if it secures the construction loan.

Who is able to Rescind a Loan?
- The Right of Rescission does not apply to just borrowers. All consumers who have an ownership interest in the property have the right to rescind.

Special Rules for Loans in Foreclosure
After initiation of foreclosure on the borrower's principal dwelling that secures the loan, the consumer can rescind if:
- A mortgage broker fee that should have been included in the finance charge was not included; or
- The creditor did not provide the right of rescission notice.

Right of Rescission Requirements for Lenders
- Lenders must provide certain "material disclosures and multiple copies of the right of rescission notice to EACH owner of the property.
- After providing all proper disclosures, lenders must wait at least 3 business days before disbursing loan proceeds.

What are the Material Disclosures?
- An accurate and complete Truth in Lending Disclosure Form.
- Disclosure must include the APR, finance charge, amount financed, and total of payments.
- Other necessary disclosures include the number of payments to be made over the life of the loan and the regular payment amount.

TILA Disclosures Must Be Accurate
Accuracy relies on two elements:
- Finance Charge
- Annual Percentage Rate, the "APR"

Finance Charge Accuracy
- If the borrower is seeking to rescind and the lender has not started foreclosure proceedings –the tolerance is one-half of one percent (.005).
- If the lender has started foreclosure proceedings, the tolerance is $35.
- If the lender overstates the Finance Charge, there is no extended right to rescind.

Annual Percentage Rate – APR Accuracy
- Tolerance for the APR disclosed in the TILA Disclosure is one-eighth of one percent (.00125).
- The APR is inaccurate if it exceeds or is lower than the true APR by .00125 (see Commentary 226.22(a)(2)-1.
- One-eighth of one percent (.00125) accuracy tolerance applies to "regular" transactions.

A Word about HOEPA Loans
- TILA was amended in 1994 to add the Home Ownership and Equity Protection Act.
- The main purpose of the law was to protect consumers from predatory lending practices.

- The law imposed new disclosure requirements and substantive limitations on certain closed-end mortgage loans bearing rates or fees above a certain percentage or amount.
- Failure to provide properly completed HOEPA Disclosures or use of a prohibited loan term can create an extended right to rescind the loan.

Rescission Process - Notifying the Lender
- Borrower must notify the lender, in writing, of the cancellation of the loan.
- Notice can be transmitted by mail, telegram, or other means.
- It should be sent to the lender's designated place of business.
- A rescission notice sent by the borrower's attorney is also effective.
- When the lender fails to provide an address to send the rescission notice, delivery to the Servicer will be effective notice as to the lender or its assignee.

Relationship between Servicer and Creditor
- 15 USC section 1641, liability of assignees (f) Treatment of servicer–(2) et seq. Upon written request by the obligor, the servicer shall provide the obligor, to the best knowledge of the servicer, with the name, address, and telephone number of the owner of the obligation or the master servicer of the obligation.

Effects of Rescission
- Once a consumer rescinds a transaction, the security interest becomes void and the consumer is not liable for ANY amount, including finance charges.
- Within 20 calendar days after receipt of a notice of rescission, the creditor shall return any money or property that has been given to anyone in connection with the loan.
- The lender must take steps to terminate the security interest.
- Once the lender has performed as above, the consumer must tender any money received back to the lender.
- Once tender is delivered, rescission is complete.

- As a result of the rescission, the lender retroactively loses the right to charge interest, fees, and costs on the loan, even costs paid to outside third parties such as the title insurer.
- Once the security interest is void, the loan is unsecured and may be included in bankruptcy. Consult an attorney.

Assignee Liability
- 15 USC section 1641, liability of assignees
- (c) Right of rescission by consumer unaffected –Any consumer who has the right to rescind a transaction under 15 USC 1635 of this title may rescind the transaction as against any assignee of the obligation.

What is Rescission?

Section Three:
The Rescission Process Must Be Followed Without Fail

1. Proper Notice of Rescission.
   This will be in the form of a letter.

2. Proper Parties to Serve Notice:
   The *proper* lender(s) (creditor) and parties must be served. In so doing, the borrower should serve:

   a. The originating lender.
      i. The borrower should refer to the original loan closing package and address the Notice of Rescission to the lender whose name and address appear on the original documents.
      ii. The borrower should refer to theHUD-1/1A Settlement Statement and if the lender listed on page one under Lender: is different than the lender in (i) immediately above, send a notice to this named lender as well.

   b. The current servicing lender.
      i. Refer to the most recent mortgage billing statement.
      ii. Even if the mortgage does not have a Mortgage Electronic Registration System "MERS" MIN number (18 digits) (MIN stands for Mortgage Identification Number), the borrower can go to MERS and search for the most current servicer on a loan by entering the borrower name and/or the property address. https://www.mers-servicerid.org/sis/. MERS is a lender nominee to facilitate the transferring of mortgage servicing on tens of millions of loans. If the loan is a MERS

loan then the most current loan servicer will be listed in the search results. If this is a different entity, notice should be served on them as well.

    c. The legal adversarial party (if applicable) in the foreclosure.
    d. The attorney for the lender.
    e. A copy of the notice should be filed with the court in which the borrower is fighting your foreclosure case.

3. Proper Service:
"To exercise the right to rescind, the consumer shall notify the creditor of the rescission by mail, telegram, or other means of written communication. Notice is considered given when mailed, or when filed for telegraphic transmission, or, if sent by other means, when delivered to the creditor's designated place of business." (Reg. Z § 226.15(a)(2) and § 226.23(a)(2))

4. The lender has 20 days from receipt of Notice to Void the Security Interest:
   - Within 20 days after receipt of a notice of rescission the Lender shall take any action necessary or appropriate to reflect the termination of any security interest created under the transaction. (15 USC § 1635(b)).

   - When a consumer rescinds a transaction, the security interest giving rise to the right of rescission becomes void, and the consumer shall not be liable for any amount, including any finance charge. (Reg. Z § 226.15(d)(1) and § 226.23(d)(1)), 15 USC § 1635(b).

   - "Within 20 calendar days after receipt of a notice of rescission, the creditor shall return any money or property that has been given to anyone in connection with the transaction and shall take any action necessary to reflect the termination of the security interest." (Reg. Z § 226.15(d)(2) and § 226.23(d)(2)), , 15 USC § 1635(b).

192

- The consumer may retain possession until the creditor has met its obligation. Tender of money must be made at the creditor's designated place of business. (Reg. Z § 226.15(d)(3) and § 226.23(d)(3)), 15 USC § 1635(b).

- Courts may modify the tender offer and return of property and crediting of money process including the 20 calendar days for response by Lender as well as any aspect of the tender offer process. (Reg. Z § 226.15(d)(4) and § 226.23(d)(4)), 15 USC § 1635(b). Courts may adjust tender and time frames, in which case the court ordered time frames preside.

  "For example, when a consumer is in bankruptcy proceedings and prohibited from returning anything to the creditor, or when the equities dictate, a modification might be made. The sequence of procedures under § 226.23(d)(2) and (3), or a court's modification of those procedures under § 226.23(d)(4), does not affect a consumer's substantive right to rescind and to have the loan amount adjusted accordingly. Where the consumer's right to rescind is contested by the creditor, a court would normally determine whether the consumer has a right to rescind and determine the amounts owed before establishing the procedures for the parties to tender any money or property." (FRB-OSC Paragraph § 226.23(d)(4))

5. The Tender Offer Process:

- When the lender has complied with the obligation to credit the money paid in by the borrower and take action to terminate the security interest as discussed in item 4 immediately above, the borrower must "tender" the adjusted balance due on the mortgage back to the lender. (Reg. Z § 226.15(d)(3) and § 226.23(d)(3)), 15 USC § 1635(b).

  ➢ **CRITICAL LENDER RESPONSE: If the creditor does not take possession of the money or property within 20 calendar days after the consumer's tender, the**

consumer may keep it without further obligation. (Reg. Z § 226.15(d)(3) and § 226.23(d)(3)), , 15 USC § 1635(b). SCAR: There are recent cases where courts have awarded borrowers their homes "free and clear" of a mortgage where the lender has not responded in the required timeframe.

This is an especially misunderstood area by many. Some attorneys and borrowers make the mistake of thinking borrowers facing foreclosure have destroyed their credit and cannot get financing to make a tender offer. The following example should help to clarify that this is not necessarily true. The following is a TILA violations only offer.

- o $300,000 loan amount.
- o Foreclosure is claiming an additional $100,000 in back payments, penalties, costs and attorney fees.
- o Lender has a foreclosure claim for $400,000.

Original loan amount:	$300,000
Lender foreclosure claims:	$100,000
Total of Lender's claims against borrower:	$400,000
TILA:	
Mortgage is void, additional lender claims void.	($100,000)
30 payments of $2,500/month Principal and Interest:	($ 75,000)
Original closing costs:	($ 8,000)
Statutory damages:	($ 2,000)
Attorney fee award:	($ 20,000)
Borrower credits to offset lender claims:	($205,000)

TILA Tender Offer: $195,000

Note: HOEPA is covered after this TILA section. However for the purpose of this example, if HOEPA was also violated in addition to TILA, the claim would essentially be doubled and the result is an additional ($105,000) deduction.

TILA & HOEPA Tender Offer:
$90,000

The question of whether a borrower will now have enough equity in their home to qualify them for high interest "hard money" loan at about sixty percent loan to value, must be considered. In this example, if the home was currently appraised at $325,000 or more, this could be a distinct possibility. The higher interest rate on a $195,000 loan might offset having a lower interest rate on a higher loan amount.

TILA Example: $195,000 @ 11% interest only = $1,787 per month
$300,000 @ 8% interest only = $2,000 per month.

TILA/HOEPA Example:
$90,000 @ 11% interest only = $857 per month
$300,000 @ 8% interest only = $2,000 per month.

A borrower may or may not be able to afford this.

Tendering with a new loan, depending on the circumstances may present a viable and realistic option. Either way, the financial offsets may be used in the form of a defensive recoupment with no statute of limitations as long as the property is still owned and in the foreclosure process.

Payment Seasoning Issue: One of the important calculations for consideration of rescission benefits is the length of time the borrower has made payments on their mortgages. For example, a borrower having made 30 monthly payments will have a significantly larger financial benefit than a borrower who made 5 payments and has been in default ever since. The reason for this is that the tender amount is reduced by the monthly payments made on the loan.

Alternative Financing Issue: Borrowers sometimes confuse the voiding of a security interest in their mortgage as walking away "free" of the obligation. This is not the case. However, where significant credits exist to a borrower, the tender offer may be substantially lower than the loan amount initially made. If one deducts finance charges paid by the borrower at closing, all the payments made by the borrower and the $2,000 statutory remedy, this may be enough for a borrower to establish strong equity in their property and get a loan either themselves or with a relative or someone else as a co-signor. Begin exploring this prospect immediately upon considering rescission possibilities. The borrower will be expected to provide financing within a specified period should the tender offer be accepted.

Chapter 18

The Qualified Written Request (QWR)

One of the first things a borrower, an attorney, or loan modification company should do for the borrower facing default, pre-foreclosure, foreclosure, or loan modification negotiations is make a Qualified Written Request (QWR) to the servicing lender.

The QWR is covered by Section 6 of RESPA which is regulated by the U.S. Department of Housing and Urban Development (HUD). More specifically the Real Estate Settlement Procedures Act, 12 U.S.C. Section 2605(e), Regulation X § 3500.21(f) and TILA 15 U.S.C. § 1601, et seq. as amended. It provides that any loan servicer may be so requested by a borrower within the first twelve months of becoming the servicer of the loan. In which case the servicer is regulated to acknowledge the request within 20 business days and must try to resolve the issue within 60 business days.

HUD puts out, on its website, www.hud.gov a standardized QWR template. Identify the borrower, loan, address and contact information. Then make the request, in the suggested format:

I am writing because:
- Describe the issue or the question you have and/or what action you believe the lender should take.
- Attach copies of any related written materials.
- Describe any conversations with customer service regarding the issue and to whom you spoke.

- Describe any previous steps you have taken or attempts to resolve the issue.
- List a day time telephone number in case a customer service representative wishes to contact you.

HUD also makes the following notes:
1. REMEMBER: This letter SHOULD NOT be included with your mortgage payment, but should be sent separately to the customer service address.
2. You SHOULD continue to make the required mortgage and escrow payment until the request is resolved.
3. You may bring a private right of action under Section 6, if you suffer damages due to the lender's servicing of the loan. See the RESPA statute and regulations.

Presumably, it is the first item which HUD advises borrowers should write about, that gives many the impression it is okay and acceptable practice to include a laundry list of allegations, complaints and demands. *"Describe the issue or the question you have and/or what action you believe the lender should take."*

The issue or the question makes it clear to the servicing lender that a laundry list of requests does not have to be answered. In response to laundry lists, lenders typically ignore or dismiss claims that go beyond the statute. It is a waste of time to put a case on hold for a couple of months expecting to receive the requested information, only to find it will not be supplied. The following information is designed to help understand the QWR and proceed accordingly.

The following reviews some concerns and discusses their appropriateness.

"My concern is potential predatory, unfair, deceptive and fraudulent misrepresentation of loan terms.
   a. Income inflated on the final printed application.
   b. Forged signatures.
   c. Lack of a witness or notary appearing in person.

d. Foreign language issues. Documents must be presented in the language you speak and understand."

The above issues appear to be loan origination based, not loan servicer based, unless the loan servicer is the loan issuer as might happen in a portfolio loan (this book is not addressing portfolio loans, but rather securitized loans).

An appropriate issue or question could include:
Questioning the debt.
a. Principal amount balance lender claims to be owed.
   i. Improper credit of payment portions to interest instead of principal
   ii. Improper late fees
   iii. Principal not reducing as per expected amortization
   iv. Amortized properly.
b. Fees or forced insurance that have been charged, collected from or assessed to the loan.
c. Calculations of the monthly payment.
   i. Increases
   ii. Interest and principal calculated and applied properly
d. Calculations of the escrow deposits and payments.
   i. Increases for fees and expenses the borrower is not legally obligated to
e. Payments properly credited to the account.
f. Account properly adjusted, debited, charged.

Another appropriate issue or question could include:
Mortgage servicing system information and data reporting on the loan, from inception of loan to date.
   a.   Include notations
   b.   Include Fidelity CPI system, Alltel, or software system reporting information.
   c.   Include legends, codes and descriptions of same if not readily apparent to the borrower.

Another appropriate issue or question could include: Loan servicing

1) All loan servicing records
2) All payoff calculations
3) All Adjustable Rate Mortgage ARM audits
4) Transaction Histories
5) Loan histories
6) Payment records,
7) Interest rate adjustments
8) Escrow account records and adjustments
9) Accounting records
10) Ledgers
11) Registers

An appropriate issue or question could include:
Proper valid payment verification of charges on my loan.
1. List all fees and expenses paid on my loan
2. Provide copies of back and front of checks
3. Provide details of debits and drafts paid on my loan
4. Written evidence of all payments
5. Invoices for charges made on my account
       A. Attorney Fees
       B. Appraisal fees
       C. Inspection fees
       D. BPO fees
       E. Insurance
       F. Taxes
       G. Assessments
       H. Any expense charged to the loan account

Other appropriate issues or questions could include:
- Escrow analysis
- If loan modifications, including deed-in-lieu and short sales have been considered or performed, included documentation.
- Document any assignment or involvement of MERS (Mortgage Electronic Registration System)

The HUD recommended format of the QWR does not include the borrower' threatening the Servicer, yet it appears from many "suggested" QWRs on blogs and the Internet, that t this is the desired purpose. It is a waste of time and very unproductive. If a QWR request has been made, then the information can be used in the Lender Compliance Analysis℠ examination process. Analysis of the mortgage history tells a lot about unfair business practices.

Author's Note on the upcoming chapters through the end of this book:

LCA and FLD

The following chapters discuss the Lender Compliance Analysis ᔆᴹ ("LCA") and Forensic Lender Discovery ᔆᴹ ("FLD") services provided by my firm, FPG-USA. Although I am sure there are other credible providers of this type of service, due to the fact that mortgage analysis and discovery is not a licensed industry, I cannot speak to the services provided by others in the field. The following pertains only to the services offered by FPG-USA.

Chapter 19

What is Lender Compliance Analysis ℠ (LCA)?

- Overview
- The Benefits of LCA
- LCA Examinations Performed
- What Loans are Covered?
- Lender Compliance Analysis ℠ (LCA) Strategy
- Important Shopping Points to Consider

Overview

Lender Compliance Analysis ℠ (LCA) is a patent pending forensic loan compliance analysis and reporting system (loan auditing). It provides in an automated method, similar examination processes that manual compliance auditors have been doing by hand for years. The service is accessible online in a do-it-yourself process designed to save users time and money, as well as provide the assistance and intervention of forensic loan experts to establish the highest level of reporting integrity.

The LCA System examines existing mortgage loans for violations of governmental regulations such as Truth in Lending Act ("TILA"), Real Estate Settlement Procedures Act ("RESPA"), Home Ownership and Equity Protection Act ("HOEPA"), and Unfair Deceptive Acts and Practices (UDAP) that may be relevant on the State level. LCA is designed to be used as part of a credible legal defense against foreclosure, pre-foreclosure, and default loan servicing, or may be used to assist in negotiating a settlement or loan modification. Depending on the loan specifics and the violations, remedies may include:

- Congressionally legislated financial offsets and setoffs in the form of defensive recoupment
- Statutory Damages
- Civil Damages
- Actual damages
- Attorneys fees and court costs
- Extended Right of Rescission

The above remedies can get a borrower out of a bad loan completely, provide significant offsets against amounts due, and / or help to promote a serious settlement negotiation with the lender/servicer if the borrower is attempting to modify the loan.

The Lender Compliance Analysis audit begins by examining several of the loan closing documents:

1) HUD-1 (or HUD-1A) Settlement Statement;
2) Truth in Lending Disclosure (all copies);
3) All disclosures received at loan closing;
4) Mortgage (1st 2 pages);
5) Note and any note riders;
6) Notice of right to cancel on refinances

These documents were issued or supposed to be issued when the borrower took out the loan.

Each analysis has the same objectives:
- Assess compliance with disclosure forms.
- Assess compliance Timing of disclosures.
- Assess use and compliance of Electronic disclosures.
- Assess compliance by performing mathematical computations on loan numbers (finance charges, annual percentage rate, adjustable rates, etc.)

There are other examination areas in the analysis as well, for example:
- Advertising requirements. Use of prohibited terms.

- Record retention. Keeping advertisement for specified times in order to have a record of possible violations that can be examined in an audit.
- Closed end mortgages
- HELOCS
- Open end mortgages

When violations are found, the following may be supplied:
- Findings Report with bona-fide discovery issues that can provide for delay and/or dismissal as well as remedies, which might include possible rescission of the mortgage.
- Pleadings from cases
- The Rules and Remedies

In examining for possible violations, each analysis includes (if applicable):
- Detailed references to Code and Act;
- Summary of questions and answers the findings are based on;
- Application and purpose of each audit Act (TILA, RESPA, HOEPA);
- Substantive requirements for consideration under the appropriate Act including triggers for coverage;
- Disclosure requirements;
- Prohibitions, material violations with code references;
- Remedies with code references;
- Possible claims for monetary damages under civil, criminal liability and administrative actions;
- Applicable statutes of limitations;
- Section with suggestions and notes, if applicable.

Critical to valuable reporting is running the various analysis checks for compliance. The difference is often in the details.

Courts are mandated to remedies in the case of many LCA violations. This means that if you have a violation, the court, under Federal and State agency regulations must follow the code and statute remedies.

That is not the same as a court action whereby the judge is going to rule one way or the other after hearing both sides. This can provide leverage in court and when applied as directed in this chapter, also in settlement.

The series of tests performed by the LCA examination are designed to run through each codified statute and identify violations in each area. Violations are a defense in foreclosure with varying remedies. Using the LCA, it is possible to run a dual track and use the report to exercise the violation remedies, as well as use the report in negotiating a loan modification with the lender at the same time.

The TILA audit process relies on established legal source(s). For example:

- 15 U.S.C. § 1601; et. Seq.
- FDIC Law, Regulations, Related Acts 6500 - Consumer Protection
- Regulation Z: part 226 - Truth in Lending [Codified to 12 C.F.R. § 226.1
- Comptroller of the Currency Administrator of National Banks; Truth in Lending,
- Comptroller's Handbook, dated accordingly.

The LCA service is designed to benefit the professionals working on a borrower's case whether it is an attorney and/or loan modification professional. The LCA audit process only requires a short list of original loan documents from the closing and provides instant results at the end of the examination. This eliminates the need to send in documentation and wait weeks for results that is common when using traditional loan audits.

Additional services, such as certification and consultation, are optional and are provided in an expedited fashion based upon the work queue at the time. In most cases, look for response within three business days after receipt of all documentation and information requested by FPG-USA staff. Rush service may be available for an additional fee.

The Benefits of LCA

Instant "do-it-yourself" Examinations

The LCA examinations analyze a loan for specific violations and remedies of the Truth in Lending Act, Home Ownership and Equity Protection Act, Real Estate Settlement Procedures Act and violation alerts on Federal Trade Commission Act (FTC Act) Unfair and Deceptive Acts and Practices Statutes as they are reflected in a specific State's consumer protection statutes. All 50 States have their own laws based on the FTC Act.

Qualifying Expert

The chapter in this book entitled Evidence vs. Hearsay illustrates the importance of providing a qualifying expert to support the foundation of providing evidence in court. Consultation services are provided on a per inquiry nominal fee basis to facilitate submission of reporting under the rules of evidence in all courts. Mortgage analysis as a credible part of a legal defense against foreclosure is subject to an individual judge's interpretation of the "expertise" in accepting reports into evidence in accordance with the rules of civil procedure and rules of evidence. A judge, or any party to the case, should be able to inquire to a senior expert on any report issued by any firm providing this type of analysis.

Suggested Cases for Attorney Review (SCARs) ˢᴹ

Attorneys often need assistance in formulating pleadings. The LCA Reports provide this in the form of Suggested Cases for Attorney Review (SCARs) ˢᴹ. SCARs ˢᴹ provide case reference information to attorneys for their consideration. SCARs ˢᴹ are generated in the reporting engine of LCA system, as well as available in the attorney access portion of the FPG-USA Library available online at www.fpg-usa.com.

SCARs ˢᴹ tend to be important legal precedent setting or affirming cases in support or of reference to the topic being reported. SCARs ˢᴹ may also include practice "tips" for attorneys.

Stair Step Pricing Structure

Firms that do not offer "stair stepped pricing" tend to take advantage of borrowers whose reporting does not produce violations at all, or violations that will likely result in insignificant financial remedies. For example, why spend hundreds of dollars to find out you only have a claim of $2,000 in statutory damages on top of legal fees and court costs? That is the case in many purchase mortgages under TILA.

FPG-USA currently employs a "stair step" approach to save borrowers money and produce instant online results. Under the LCA system, every loan added undergoes a free coverage test. If coverage applies, loan information may be input and the entire process of examinations can be taken online. The result is an Assessment. If the assessment finds violations, a Report can be ordered. The Report contains the violation reporting in a form required for submission as evidence to court or a lender's legal department if the purpose is loan modification negotiations.

If rescission is applicable, an instant customized Rescission Package is available for a nominal charge. The documents in this package are fully customized to the specific loan and supplied immediately online in a ready to print, address, sign, date, and mail form. Rescission Package documents cite specific violations and include a Cancellation Letter, Notice and Demand for Rescission and Tender Offer with financial calculations.

If a court or lender requires it, a staff expert can certify any issuance, reviewing the documentation used in the examinations. If a judge or lender requires questioning a qualifying expert on a particular loan issuance either in the process of establishing an evidence foundation or for any other reason, the borrower's attorney can arrange a phone conference call with the judge and/or parties and a qualifying expert for a nominal charge to satisfactorily answer all questions posed.

In this manner, borrowers pay only for services they require. Excellence of service, quality and customer satisfaction should be an important consideration in choosing a mortgage analysis firm.

Calculating return on Investment

Every borrower and / or borrower's attorney should be able to evaluate the potential benefits sought against the cost. Analysis and reporting is only one part of the equation and represents only a fraction of the costs including legal and professional fees. Borrowers can generally expect to pay an attorney a reasonable fee for each step performed in the LCA process. Assessment, Reporting, Rescission Package, each require time, effort and expense by the professional ordering services. This is to be expected. Firms should be upfront with their fees and have no hidden charges. LCA fees and associated services are posted clearly at www.fpg-usa.com.

LCA Examinations Performed

Here is a sample of the examinations performed, as applicable, on loans submitted to FPG-USA's Lender Compliance Analysis ˢᴹ System.

Truth in Lending Act (TILA)
- Payment Period Disclosure
- ARM Payment Schedule Start Rate Deception
- Finance Charge Tolerance and Violation
- Extended Right of Rescission
- One Year For Affirmative Claims
- In Foreclosure Affirmative Claims
- APR Tolerance
- Loan Coverage
- TIL Disclosure Issuance
- Negative Amortization Disclosure
- Consumer Handbook on Adjustable Rate Mortgage Disclosure
- Rescission Notice Delivery
- Rescission Receipt Acknowledged
- Rescission Notice Made Conspicuously

Real Estate Settlement Procedures Act (RESPA)
- Loan Coverage
- Special Information Booklet
- Good Faith Estimate (GFE)
- Hud-1/1a Uniform Settlement Statement
- Hud-1/1a Prohibition of Fees
- Title Company
- Mortgage Servicing Transfer Notice
- Qualified Written Request

Unfair, Deceptive Acts and Practices (UDAP) as reflected in all 50 States, including D.C. and Puerto Rico's consumer protection laws.

- Loan Proceeds Test
- Property taxes due paid at closing
- Home Improvement Paid at Closing
- Existing loan payoff
- Deceptive Mortgage Broker Fee
- Payment Posting
- Excessive settlement charges
- Blatant Forgery
- Equity Stripping
- Bait and Switch
- Forced placed insurance
- Income Exaggeration
- Mandatory Arbitration Clause
- Foreign Language Deception

Home Ownership and Equity Protection Act (HOEPA)

- APR Tolerance
- Points and Fees Tolerance
- Coverage
- Pre-consummation Waiting Period
- Lose Your Home Notice
- Balloon Payment
- Higher Default Interest Rate
- Prepayment Penalty Disclosures
- Due-on-Demand Feature Disclosure
- Repayment Ability
- Refinance Within One Year
- Evasion; Open-end Credit
- Negative Amortization

What Loans are Covered?

LCA examinations apply to mortgages secured by residential real estate on property secured by personal loans for family purposes.

Foreclosure

If the loan is currently in a foreclosure proceeding there is no statute of limitations on offsets in the form of defensive recoupment, meaning amounts that are credited against the lenders accounting claims of amounts owed.

Refinances and Home Equity Loans

The Extended Right of Rescission is the most powerful remedy available under TILA and HOEPA and is available in foreclosure and out of foreclosure but it is limited to refinances and home equity loans that are less than three years old.

Half of the power is derived from the sheer dollar amounts because it credits all payments made on the loan, all pre-paid finance charges, actual and civil damages as well as attorney fees and court costs.

The other half of the power is the rescission which voids the underlying security interest in a loan. In addition to the well established rescission benefits, some attorneys feel that loans rendered unsecured may be dischargeable in Chapter 13 bankruptcy. This issue has proponents on both sides of the fence.

However, the power of rescission has long been established relative to any court. Borrowers must "tender" an offer to the lender, which is reduced by all the amounts mentioned above on TILA claims and the borrower is entitled to essentially "double up" those amounts if HOEPA and TILA violations are found on the same loan. The financial benefits can be significant.

Purchases

Purchases have limited dollar amount benefits of $2,000 per loan in statutory civil damages <u>unless actual damages can be proven</u>. The $2,000 is on the entire transaction, no matter how many violations are found. Of course, court costs and attorney fees 15 U.S.C. § 1640(a) applies if the case is won.

Actual damages are hard to prove because courts may require the borrower to show they relied on the accuracy of the disclosures and if they had actually been accurate, the borrower would have sought out and taken a better loan. Actual damages can be significant depending on the difference in interest rates and fees and the subsequent overall savings. In addition, negative amortization claims can play an important role. In a negative amortization loan, the original principal amount can grow and eventually contribute the property being "upside down" meaning the mortgage is more than the home is worth and prevent refinancing, so that the borrower is stuck in a position that forces foreclosure if the payments as they stand cannot be made.

Negative amortization loans compared to traditional amortization can result in actual damages of the negative amounts added to the original loan amount, plus claims resulting from the loan being upside down. In these cases, actual damages can be substantial and as such, can put a purchase loan into a very favorable position under the regulations to make substantial borrower financial claims as an offset against lender claims in the form of defensive recoupment. In foreclosure there is no statute of limitations. Outside of foreclosure, purchase mortgages are limited to a one year statute of limitations from date of loan closing to be eligible for affirmative claims (15 U.S.C. § 1640(e)).

Loan Assignment or Sale Does Not Matter
Borrowers with violations reporting have protections that cover them even if the loan has been assigned or sold after the closing to another lender or even to subsequent lenders over time. Liability under TILA where the violation is apparent on the face of the loan documents because claims for monetary damages, runs against assignees (15 U.S.C. § 1641(a)). "Any consumer who has the right to rescind a transaction under section 1635 of this title may rescind the transaction as against any assignee of the obligation" (15 U.S.C. § 1641(c)).

Lender Compliance Analysis ^{SM} (LCA) Strategy

LCA Reporting is a service attorneys usually implement in the following way:

1. Perform a FREE Coverage Exam. If the loan qualifies,
2. Run through the examination series and receive an Assessment.
3. If the Assessment shows violations:
4. Order and print a Report. If rescission (cancellation of the loan) is a remedy,
5. Order and print the customized ready to go Rescission Package
6. If in a lawsuit, submit the findings into evidence.
7. If not yet in a lawsuit, submit the findings to lender's legal dept. with a letter of intent.
8. If challenged and expert is required, set up a conference call with the FPG-USA expert.
9. Proceed with forensic lender discovery.
10. Proceed with filing or answering complaint if applicable.
11. Proceed with first requests for admissions, interrogatories and document discovery.
12. Try to settle a good loan modification. For example:
    a. Loan amount to 80% LTV
    b. Payments to 31% back end ratio
    c. Term: 30 to 40 years fixed
    d. Payments made by lender for taxes and insurance: Added to back of loan.
    e. Fees and penalties, waived.
    f. Credit, reported to zero late payments.
13. If lender is not true owner with standing to foreclose, move for dismissal.

Loan modification professionals who are in the process before an actual foreclosure action is implemented, may order mortgage analysis on behalf of the borrowers and use violations in their negotiations. The borrower is also free to take this report if so desired, and use it in the process of finding an attorney if needed down the road, and provide the report issuances to the attorney for use on the borrower's behalf. There are no additional FPG-USA fees associated with this process unless the attorney wishes to implement additional services beyond what have been ordered. In this way, a borrower can get more mileage out of the reporting process in the form of gaining an advantage in a loan modification negotiation as well as in a legal proceeding.

Borrowers should absolutely and unequivocally seek professional legal advice. Many attorneys do not provide loan modification services in their legal foreclosure defense services. Loan modification is a time consuming affair.

Short Sales. A very useful strategy of realtors in the process of short sale negotiations is to order mortgage analysis for leverage in the negotiation process. The issuances can be used subsequently by the borrower as described above.

Chapter 20

What is Forensic Lender Discovery ^{SM} (FLD)?

The "show me the note" defense made popular with widespread news coverage is one example of literally dozens of potential areas of mortgage "toxicity". This chapter will cover the process of examining a loan for toxicity via FPG-USA's Forensic Lender Discovery SM ("FLD") process. FLD is a very powerful resource for the borrower's attorney facing foreclosure. It may also be used by Investors, Trusts and Trustees who have been hurt financially in the securitization process.

FLD examines the institutional securitization (sale of the loan in pools to investors) aspect of a mortgage looking for toxicity, flaws in the mortgage that would undermine the right to foreclosure. It is not the examination of the documentation leading up to the closing. That aspect of loan analysis is performed by the Lender Compliance Analysis SM system covered in the previous chapter.

People or groups using FLD will generally fall into these categories.
1. The individual borrower fighting foreclosure.
2. The investor in a mortgage pool fighting loss.
3. The Trustee of an investor trust seeking class action damages.
4. Institutional purchasers of MBSs seeking class action damages.
5. Class action parties seeking damages against institutional, corporate, banking, insurance, securities and other parties and counterparties involved in the securitization process.

This chapter will present an overview of each category.

Category 1: The individual borrower fighting foreclosure

Every case that is considered for an FLD should, in all instances, perform an LCA examination prior to considering the FLD. At FPG-USA this is a requisite to every FLD request. FLD covers many loans and situations that LCA does not cover, but in no circumstance is FLD a substitute for a case that qualifies for LCA governmental agency violation remedies. (See previous chapter for LCA information).

Borrowers should not go Pro Se

The process of using FLD usually involves a legal action. Borrowers often inquire about FLD under the pretense that they will use the reporting to fight their case in court under the rules of Pro Se, meaning to defend one self.

This is surprising and scary, considering the borrower did not have the necessary skills to avoid taking a predatory loan out in the first place. Borrowers should hire competent legal representation. Presuming that a borrower landed themselves in the untenable position of a mortgage facing foreclosure and was not able to negotiate a loan modification, the consideration of mounting a successful legal defense is tantamount to legal and financial suicide. In many cases, the loss of a home and the claims of an unsatisfied mortgage are likely the single biggest financial transaction in the borrower's present circumstances. To risk losing this is simply preposterous. Borrowers should hire an attorney who is knowledgeable in this industry to represent them if they hope to have a chance.

Against Summary Judgment

Raising material toxic issues and making first discovery requests can effectively shift the burden of proof to the Lender's shoulders. As was explained in the Evidence vs. Hearsay chapter, credibility of evidence, availability of expert testimony, and case presentation must be considered. Assuming the proper timing and steps are followed, the result of initial assessment and response to first requests will enable a credible mortgage analysis company to perform preliminary forensic findings of mortgage toxicity and come up with material issues.

This is a critical crossroads in every case. In shifting the burden to the Lender, they are forced to answer the requests and assessment findings. Any attempt to avoid or lie about issues must be confronted. The Judge may have to step in, either on their own or by request and force the lender to answer honestly. This step is usually enough to move the case into serious loan modification settlement negotiations with a strict time period based on the time limit to which the answers are required in the court process. Now, the borrower's attorney is moving down a dual track; one to defeat foreclosure and one to settlement. Thus the lender hold is reversed.

This course of action will likely prevent the immediate result of a lender winning Summary Judgment at the outset against a borrower being represented by competent counsel. It should be noted however, that up against a borrower fighting their own case Pro Se, or an incompetent attorney, even powerful material issues may not prevent losing to Summary Judgment.

NRM Lender foreclosure attorneys know all the tricks and wield them well. A competent borrower's attorney must cite legal precedent that will prevent Summary Judgment against the borrower from taking place before the information requested is supplied to the satisfaction of the mortgage analysis firm requesting it.

Judges are careful to follow guiding legal case precedent to avoid being overturned on appeal. However, this is a judge's prerogative and realm. The important thing is not to submit material that is non-essential or not required. The material presented should be easy and straightforward for the judge. Attorneys should stick to the facts and material issues that are pertinent to the case and not objectionable in the form submitted. This is one of the rules of evidence in many states. Experts will know the form of submitting material facts. Objectionable is left to the Judge's interpretation but slander, accusations without evidence, use of inappropriate language or subject matter may all safely be assumed to be included in the term "objectionable".

Do not let the dual tracks of settlement and foreclosure trick you. Lenders operate on dual tracks in foreclosure cases. On the one hand moving to foreclose and on the other hand seeming to be considering a loan modification to save or sell.

An example would be one we which is seen in the business all the time. The court case is moving on a fast tract, motions are being entered in court for summary judgment and default judgments. At the same time the attorney and borrower are eagerly awaiting some response to short sale offers or loan modification settlement offer answers. The borrower and their attorney are in contact with the lender's loss mitigation department on the short sale and settlement and expecting rapid response. They are cautioned not to upset the possibility of a settlement or acceptance with aggressive opposition in court.

Unfortunately, in the process of waiting for an answer the case may be lost in court because the borrower's attorney was taken in by the process of settlement negotiations. It is imperative for the borrower's attorney to stay on the dual track with as much attention to the foreclosure case as is required to keep it on the borrower's track of winning against foreclosure.

Settlement Options Can Appear Where They Didn't Exist Before. Whether it is the loan modification professional who attaches a verifiable findings report in the process of negotiation, the person attempting to have a short sale accepted or the attorney representing the borrower in foreclosure, the competent professional will be in contact with the Lender's legal department as well as the lender's loss mitigation department.

The purpose of credible mortgage analysis is enabling both sides to properly assess the lender's vulnerability according to the findings. Unfortunately, at the time of this writing, many lenders are not settling well with borrowers but are rather attempting to foreclose. This is understandable knowing the risks lenders face in a securitized transaction loan modification.

1. When loans modify, some investors in the mortgage pool benefit and some are hurt. The fear is from a class action by the ones hurt in the process.
2. The Trustee in the mortgage pool representing investors may be looking for recourse from the originating lender. Getting out of the risk of lawsuit is generally accomplished with a foreclosure.
3. Loan modification produces little profit to the lender in comparison to the windfall profit of winning a home in foreclosure, especially where compensating factors have repaid the mortgage holder in full or part.
4. When the servicing lender is a sub-servicer, the process of transiting the national loan servicing platform structure up through the servicing entities to the master servicer and then to the Trustee of the investors for approval, can be a burdensome task for a servicer whose staff is already under maximum workload. Logistics problems can be complicated with interim lenders and servicers being out of business as a result of the meltdown crisis of 2008.
5. If the loan was not properly assigned and endorsed on the face of the note, it may be considered defective under the pooling and servicing agreement of the securitized transaction and may be subject to a mandatory buy back at full mortgage loan sale value. This would include any credit enhancements that may have caused the Trust to pay more than the loan face value. The result of buying a defaulted loan in or facing foreclosure could lock the lender into exorbitant losses and also open the lender to the possibility of more than the subject loan coming into scrutiny.

All in all, faced with substantial perceived potential liability that exceeds the potential rewards of pursuing foreclosure, the borrower may actually receive a good loan modification that was not "on the table" before.

Toxicity Can Prevent Foreclosure

Legal impediments in the form of forensic evidence of mortgage toxicity may make it simply impossible for the Lender to foreclose. Lender Compliance Analysis ^{SM} and Forensic Lender Discovery ^{SM} may be used to aggressively leverage the borrower's position.

In the case of FLD Report of Toxicity and First Requests of discovery, the truthful responses may be too incriminating. Not supplying distinct answers within the allotted time frame established by the rules of civil procedure, or even worse, upon being ordered by the judge, may result in Summary Judgment against the lender.

Judges will not tolerate avoidance of an order to produce. So the lender is "damned if they do and damned if they don't". Even if the lender sells or otherwise transfers the mortgage servicing to another entity, the original mortgage analysis firm's work will still apply and the new case will again be forced to move sideways in court until the information as requested is supplied by the lender.

Setoffs and Offsets in the Nature of a Defensive Recoupment.

The ultimate goal of FLD discovery includes being able to reliably calculate financial profits that have not been divulged to the court or borrower.

Another goal is evidencing that the NRM lender was not acting as a lender at all but merely acting as a broker because they immediately sold the loan and did not have one cent of lending risk in the loan. Profits in the form of points and fees earned brokering loans are strictly limited by the TILA[31] and HOEPA[32] and UDAP[33]. NRM Lender's claiming to be lending when in reality they are merely brokering may expose themselves to significant financial setoffs or offsets in the nature of defensive recoupment and disgorgement of profits.

---

[31] Truth in Lending Act
[32] Home Ownership and Equity Protection Act. Section 32 of TILA
[33] Unfair, Deceptive Acts and Practices. All 50 states have consumer protection laws in this area, but all states are not equal in their coverage, violations and remedies.

This is another solid reason to submit Lender Compliance Analysis ^{SM} in every case, to notice the Judge on the limits of TILA and HOEPA on points and fees and the relation to Unfair and Deceptive Acts and Practices in earning more than the guidelines allow brokers and lenders to operate under. Remember, TILA <u>mandates</u> Judge's actions, with little or no "wiggle" room in most cases. In this way the LCA can be used as a benchmark.

The little known risk to a Lender: Buying back the loan.
If the loan was not properly assigned and endorsed on the face of the note, it may be considered defective under the pooling and servicing agreement of the securitized transaction and may be subject to a mandatory buy back at full mortgage loan sale value.

This is one of the most feared risks to a lender discovered to have not properly transferred the notes and ownership along to the investor in the form and within the prescribed time limits (for example, 60 to 180 days) required by the federally filed pooling and servicing agreements,. This would force the lender to buy back the loan at its face value or even worse, if sold to the trust at an inflated value.

No lender wants to be forced by a pooling and servicing agreement clause to buy back a mortgage facing foreclosure at face value. The facts are clearly damning. If the servicing lender, who is claiming they have the right to foreclose, is immediately required to buy the mortgage back if it was not transferred properly, they wouldn't have the right to foreclose that they are claiming. They would have to first buy the mortgage back from the investor pool, properly transfer it back and only then begin the foreclosure process. This would be the correct and legitimate process.

In reality, this logical and fair outcome is a nightmarish thought for the NRM Lender caught red handed. Instead of receiving a windfall profit of a foreclosure sale on top of already receiving payment in full for the mortgage at origination and the profits of selling and reselling it in CDOs, and receiving Credit Default Swap premiums over an extended period, the lender has to immediately refund the mortgage amount back to the investors.

Given a choice, no lender wants to buy a mortgage back at full face value and take back a mortgage on a property worth less than the property itself with a borrower who can only afford the mortgage if it is crammed down in a loan modification. The fact the lender was paid in full for that loan already is no consolation.

If the Trustee of the pool does not cause the repurchase to transpire, the *Trustee* now becomes in breach and the entire pool of investors can undergo a class action against the Trustee and the Lender for failure to do so.

It is fully disclosed when NRM Lenders , Trustees and other parties to the securitized mortgage transaction are non-arms length parties. Judges and attorneys can naturally expect some difficulty in making one friendly party "bite" the other financially. Make no mistake about it, the responsibilities of a pool Trustee, usually a huge investment banking firm, are to the Investor first and foremost.

A judge faced with this scenario might dismiss the case without prejudice, enabling the case to be brought back at a later date. The court in this case does not have jurisdiction until such time as the rightful owner clears up their issues and comes back with a proper case. Those bringing actions under the Rules of Civil Procedure cannot simply switch parties to suit their situation mid-stream in a case. The case would have to be closed and a new one opened. This can add significant time elements to the case.

Ownership, standing and jurisdiction must be established first.
On this topic of ownership, it may likely be discovered that the Trust has not evidenced the undisputable right of ownership, required to bring a foreclosure case in court. A Judge may be led to believe the investors of a particular pool paid good money for the mortgage. But the UCC and State rules require proof of ownership being demonstrated, not merely alleged.

If the note is being alleged as lost or stolen, this should be immediately suspected. In the process of securitization explained in previous chapters, this document was very likely specifically and properly transferred to the Document Custodian with certifications and attestations made to that effect. Top accounting or legal firms may have also been involved with confirming the receipt of the properly transferred original note and may have made and filed sworn federal statements to this effect. When this documentation is present in a securitized transaction, and the Document Custodian is not the entity making the claim, it is a powerful indication of toxic ownership issues that merit further investigation.

Indemnification

Lenders will claim to indemnify in foreclosure where the lender cannot produce the original note. What use is indemnification when lenders are folding like houses of cards, if they do not put the full loan amount into an escrow account or post a bond? It may be years before the holder of the original note comes around seeking to take possession of the property. This has been known to happen. Giving foreclosure ownership to a lender in which discovery puts the ownership into question and all the proper avenues of inquiring after the original note through the Document Custodian have not been investigated, is simply wrong. The Document Custodian sections of this book illustrate the serious nature of this responsibility and the paper trail in the process. It is a sad day when a court plays directly into the hands of deceptive misrepresentation by an NRM Lender to essentially steal a home in foreclosure from a borrower that has been issued a predatory loan for that purpose.

If these lenders are forced to answer the First Requests and subsequent discovery is performed, it is a relatively straightforward process to trace the transaction through the securitization process and find the note. Document Custodians must report these types of losses and carry insurance against them. It is more than a matter of complacent allegations, this type of loss should be proven beyond a shadow of a doubt before the court effects what is ostensibly an eviction to unconscionably award a home in foreclosure to an NRM Lender that states they were in possession of the properly transferred original note and lost it. How did they become in possession of this from the Document Custodian? This is preposterous to anyone who understands securitization. At the very least, every step in the process of tracking the whereabouts of the original note, confirming the loss from the Document Custodian and filing insurance claims against that entity, requiring affidavits from those in contact with the note on the Document Custodian side, should be undertaken. The same steps taken in the chain of title process should be taken in the process of confirming a lost note request. It should not be allowed to materialize from thin air with no efforts made to trace the history of possession.

NRM Lender's attorneys may refer to a pooling and servicing agreement that states they were given the right to foreclose by the Trust and Investor. This being the case, there may be little doubt of that right if the mortgage and note have been properly transferred according to the law.

At the very least, on a lost or stolen note foreclosure, it may be prudent for a court to order proper discovery, or the borrower's attorney to conduct it, to produce the paper trail with appropriately signed affidavits from properly and timely involved parties who may also be deposed. Judges may not choose to award a foreclosure to an NRM Lender where initial compliance analysis and discovery in evidence shows significant questions, without proper confirmation.

NRM Lenders making the statement that a pooling and servicing agreement provides them rights of the Investor owners to foreclosure on their behalf, may be putting the cart before the horse. No rights are given if there is an improperly transferred mortgage. In fact, on an improperly transferred mortgage there is an automatic "trigger" that immediately and without another alternative, "puts" the mortgage back to the originating lender. The originating lender is obligated to buy this mortgage back upon discovery of this defective loan transfer.

Everyone understands the haste originating lenders had in realizing all the money literally "shoveled" to them by investors and Wall Street.

But nowhere does that lust for earnings negate the requirement to properly transfer the mortgage and note as specified in the pooling and servicing agreement. Nowhere does it say the court should award ownership away from the investors who paid for it and own the mortgage. And nowhere does it say the court may come in, ignore the written federally sworn pooling and servicing affidavit instructions that the NRM Lender should buy back the mortgage and to the very opposite extreme, relieve the NRM Lender of that responsibility and on top, give them the windfall profit of a home in foreclosure, an escape from the pooling agreement and sever the responsibility the NRM Lender has to the investors because that is what the foreclosure does. This is very surprising and disturbing to anyone who understands the process. It is hard to acknowledge the validity of a case so adjudicated. If this were the case in criminal cases, where a judge or judges were found to be ruling incorrectly from the bench for whatever reason, those criminal cases might be brought back for retrial. This is a very serious issue. There are millions of homes sitting in the real estate owned divisions of these NRM Lenders that haven't been sold. Even if a home taken in this manner has been sold, one would suspect down the road to see actions to correct this judicial mistake.

Continuing with the specter of a forced buyback of the defaulted mortgage, the NRM Lender caught red handed can be forced with the written proclamation of the pooling and servicing agreement by serving the Trustee with formal notice of the breach. Simply reference the lender's Sale Agreement to the Trust, under which the Trustee must cause the immediate repurchase to transpire.

FLD can produce the aforementioned facts and they can be submitted into evidence by the borrower's attorney. Judges do not appreciate frivolous lawsuits. Their caseloads are burdensome. Judges have the option to decide to teach lessons to prevent the outright lies and manipulation of the court and punish this type of behavior. But first judges have to understand it. The borrower's attorney can accomplish this by submitting the evidentiary findings into evidence and requesting judicial notice under the Rules of Evidence. Provide this book to a judge if desired and set up a conference call interview with the author and expert witness for a nominal fee.

As concerns the following:
2. The investor in a mortgage pool fighting loss.
3. The Trustee of an investor trust seeking class action damages.
4. Institutional purchasers of MBSs seeking class action damages.
5. Class action parties seeking damages against institutional, corporate, banking, insurance, securities and other parties and counterparties involved in the securitization process.

After reading the above sections pertaining to borrowers, it becomes obvious that those in numbers two through five (above) have options against the NRM Lender that they may not have explored. Namely, requiring the NRM Lender under the agreements to refund the money paid on mortgages that were not properly transferred. This is a very powerful and effective workaround to the NRM Lender's sophisticated bankruptcy protection setup.

In addition, there are parties to the transaction with deep pockets who may be enjoined in a lawsuit. While investors do not have the same rights as consumers to government protection, the legal system still provides remedies.

Do not forget the Ratings Agencies (Standard & Poor's, Moody's and Fitch for example). Please refer back to the Special Purpose Vehicle diagram section and CDO Manager section. These deal with the collateralized debt obligations, the credit default swaps and the credit ratings and Meltdown 2008. From the actions, or rather inactions of the credit ratings agencies, there may be some legal and financial responsibility there. The credit agencies were not as smart as the NRM Lenders who created bankruptcy and criminal action remote interim entities that performed their jobs then disappeared, nowhere to be found, no one to find. To find them, go to a credible forensic mortgage analysis firm.

Chapter 21

The Forensic Lender Discovery ^{SM} Process

There are actually two distinct services FPG-USA offers in the FLD process. There is the
- automated FLD system (patent pending) available online at www.fpg-usa.com; and
- manual processes.

The automated FLD System:
In much the same way as the online automated LCA System is usable, the FLD System is usable. The salient points are this.
- The system is available online 24/7
- An assessment examination can be performed.
- A Findings Report can be ordered.
- First Requests for admissions, interrogatories and document discovery can be ordered.
- Additional services can be ordered as well

The automated FLD System takes the user through a series of examinations and in the end produces an assessment. The actual number of examinations and tests are case and answer driven. There are well over one hundred tests in the automated FLD System, the actual number on an individual case will vary. All examinations performed will be itemized with results in the report issuance. Based upon the assessment, a report can be ordered. Based upon the report initial first requests can be customized and selected. Like the LCA, stair stepped pricing is offered based on the services ordered. The three basic initial services are designed in total to be affordable to any borrower facing foreclosure.

The automated system is basically designed to be a quick "down and dirty" way to assess securitization toxicity that may undermine the party seeking to foreclose. It also puts findings in an evidentiary report format suitable for submission into evidence where it can shift the burden of proof to the lender on the material issues raised. The first requests can be submitted in the case. All issuances provide online verification so the court and lender's legal department see the issuances are from a legitimate mortgage analysis firm (third party).

What are Some of the Things Examined in the FLD Process?

Forensic mortgage compliance analysis and discovery is not a regulated professionally licensed industry with uniform standards as it should be. Establishing standards would immediately bring allof the things spoken about in this book to the forefront of understanding and add transparency for regulatory clarity of existing consumer protections.

Full Manual Evidentiary Findings Reports are very much on a case by case basis. For a general idea as to some things of interest a Full Evidentiary FLD Findings Report may consider are:

Identifying parties to the securitized transaction. A flow chart will include Originating Lender, Sponsor, and Depositor, SPV, Document Custodian, Trustee, Underwriter, Master Servicer and other parties including Hedge Fund Counterparties. Individual company names, addresses and key contact individuals with their titles may be supplied. It will define the roles played by each and mention specific references to these from sworn affidavit filings, so there is no question to the validity. These were provided these in the diagrams section of this book.

The report would then trace each sale of the mortgage and identify the buyers and their subsequent actions and responsibilities in the process.

Where appropriate, specific departments and contact information such as fax, phone and email, would be provided. The report will:

A. **Analyze the securitized** mortgage backed transaction documents including but not limited to sworn Securities and Exchange Commission ("SEC") filings, affidavits and reports; recognized ratings agency reports; sworn Prospectus and Pooling Agreement Filings; Management and Accounting reports and other publicly available information.

B. **Investigate and provide relevant evidence and facts** to prove or disprove Lender's allegations of material facts with ready capable determination by resorting to sources whose accuracy cannot be questioned or subject to dispute.

C. **Provide opinion and inference on the ultimate issue(s)** not intended to be objectionable because it includes issues to be decided by the Trier of fact.

D. **Provide an Executive Summary** wherein the undisputable facts are presented in a discussion format of material issues with footnotes in reference. The actual discussion on a particular case will depend on the particular findings.

E. **The facts or data submitted in the case will be of the type reasonably relied upon by experts in the subject to support the opinion expressed.** The findings report will contain the facts or data, and specific references including verbiage, location and the pertinent document where it may be found.

F. **The process investigates documentation from the closing of the particular mortgage being investigated, through securitization into a pool of mortgages, all the way up to the current servicing of the mortgage.** It does not include investigation of the origination side of the transaction, which is covered under the Lender Compliance Analysis audits in a previous chapter.

Initial documentation required from the borrower and/or their attorney:
- The court pleadings in the case
- Copies of the mortgage (or deed of trust)
- Any legal or official papers received from the lender and/or their attorney
- The court docket, if there is one

Documentation Reviewed and Form of Submission. In a full FLD Report all documents reviewed will be listed in the report and stored in a digital format. References and excerpts of the documentation will be used in the report as necessary.

Relatively little documentation is required by the borrower. The expert will acquire and review literally hundreds and sometimes over one thousand pages of documentation. There are companies online that sell much of the documentation. Before you buy any of it, which then has to be examined, your expert may already possess or have access to these documents through services they belong to, without a lot of additional document charges to the borrower. Additionally, some documentation may be found online.

The types of documents the expert will review in a full discovery may include, but are not limited to: Sworn SEC filings: Filed prospectuses, filed Polling and Servicing Agreements, 8k, 10k, Reporting Agency (S&P, Moody's, Fitch) reports, sworn accounting and legal affidavits, State, Federal and Agency. Knowing which of the thousands of pages of government and conventional single and multi family lending guidelines and forms apply, such as those of Fannie Mae, Freddie Mac, MPF, FHA, RHS, VA, MIs, GNMA, Approved Projects, Federal Compliance, plus State Compliance Guideline, helps a lot. As does familiarity with actual laws and compliance regulations for the property's state including the collection of underwriting and insuring guidelines; the State-specific disclosures and agency forms modified for use in the property's state; the relevant sections of the

Code for Federal Regulations and Federal Register; the IRS code and publications, and more.

Other services may be optionally acquired, at the discretion of the party ordering the discovery. For example, if it is suspected that a signature on an affidavit may be false, the person ordering the discovery and/or their attorney, will determine if they are going to hire a handwriting analysis expert. In a recently performed, it was possible to locate a verifiable signature of the <u>real</u> party whose signature would have appeared on a genuine affidavit, and it was so obviously different from the party of the same name and corporate position that was "claiming" to be that person on the affidavit that anyone looking at the signatures could see the difference. The affidavit was notarized and filed in the state court system and verified to be made by the real person.

Chapter 22

Forensic Lender Discovery^{SM} and Mortgage Toxicity

"Toxicity" is the degree to which flaws in a mortgage (or mortgages) can undermine claims and rights of the mortgage holder.

Toxicity and Some of the Many Forms it can Take.

Lenders commonly commit misrepresentation and both intrinsic and extrinsic fraud. Their risk is minimal if caught. When a case is simply dismissed without prejudice, Lenders are free to come back and try again. Is that a deterrent to lying? No. Hopefully that will change as the Court system learns more about seeking the facts of toxicity in the securitized mortgage transaction underlying the loan before them.

Toxicity and a Sampling of Areas Where It Can Manifest.

The "toxicity" facts presented in the evidentiary findings report should not be subject to dispute because they are capable of accurate and ready determination by referring to sources whose accuracy cannot be questioned. An example of this would be sworn affidavits, such as those that may be submitted to the Securities and Exchange Commission ("SEC"). Or sworn attested filings of an accounting and/or legal firm, or any party to the securitized mortgage transaction.

Some examples of the types of toxicity an FLD Assessment and Reports might produce or bring into questions might be finding evidence that:

- the court does not have jurisdiction in the case.
- the mortgage was actually paid in full.
- the original lender trying to foreclose actually sold the mortgage and is not the "Master Servicer" with the rights to foreclosure on behalf of the real owner.
- the current owner of the note cannot be identified.
- there were real estate transfers that were not properly affected, which may undermine the ability to foreclose under state laws.
- the lender/servicer was predatory.
- the lender has had similar cases dismissed for similar reasons in other courts.
- the loan losses were insured and perhaps collected on.
- the loan was sold for tremendous profits, potentially many times the face amount of the mortgage and this fact has not only been kept from the court, it has been intentionally hidden.
- false affidavits have been submitted to the court, perpetrating misrepresentation and fraud.
- the investor owning this mortgage was already reimbursed for the loss and paid off for all or part of this particular mortgage.
- the lender/servicer has not divulged that the extent to which it will receive proceeds from the sale of foreclosure and clearly identify amounts the true investor owner will receive.
- the Lender willfully and with knowledgeably, previously made material misrepresentations in this case to the court.
- this Lender has made misrepresentations that when taken in the context of laws, acts and a regulation of Congressional mandate to protect the borrower consumer, has lied and in so doing has committed fraud upon the court.

Intrinsic fraud is the *subject* of the lawsuit, for example, a lender providing the "original" mortgage and note as evidence of *current* ownership, claiming falsely to the court that they are the current properly transferred originals. The court is looking for the current owner's original. The lender and their attorney know the law. They are simply lying. Lender strategy employs a similar naming convention to further confuse and obfuscate the issue and make discovery of this lie that much more difficult.

Extrinsic fraud is not coming forth with the information or hiding information that would allow the borrower, their mortgage analysis firm and/or the court to obtain the information or get evidence to defend their position in the foreclosure lawsuit. This could be many things. For example: Not answering the First Requests for information, destroying the current original note; not advising the court this note was sold; not providing the court with the entity contact information that is currently holding the properly transferred originals for the current owner; not coming up with the profit side of the balance sheet in counting what the borrower owes on the mortgage and hiding profits made that should be offsets to the foreclosure calculations of amounts due in the nature of defensive recoupment; to name a few.

Misrepresentation can take many forms, such as: Falsely misstating facts, failure to properly account, claiming they have the right to foreclose when they don't, failing to produce records when the attorney knows they exist and how to obtain them, hiding income that would go against expenses, lying to the court, saying that they are communicating with a borrower on a loan modification when they have demonstrated the opposite by lack of communication and failure to present settlement offers, failing to rescind a mortgage when evidence is provided under the law and proper request is made, and scheming to defraud.

Vacating an order for Summary Judgment.
The only way to overturn the Summary Judgment is to find that undisputable fraud and misrepresentation was committed by the Lender as the basis for winning in Summary Judgment. The extra burden of evidentiary findings requires additional costs. The level of expertise required for this type of discovery is very high and the amount of time and intensity of the research justifies the added charges.

Toxicity of failing to properly account: In a typical foreclosure case, the lender is itemizing amounts owed to it on the mortgage by providing only <u>one</u> side of the accounting sheet; the debit side. What about the other side? In every case of a securitized subprime mortgage that was included in a pool there is a profit side which may include:

- Any sales of this mortgage to other parties in the form of Collateralized Debt Obligations;

- Any financial benefits this mortgage provided as a collateralized asset where a sale was not made but the mere pledging of this mortgage became an asset source of additional monies and enabled additional profits to the parties;

- Amounts realized in "up-tranching" this mortgage into a group of higher credit rated mortgage groups, earning lenders tremendous profits on subsequent sale.

- All the records of these accountings are meticulously maintained by parties to the transactions and certified by top accounting firms. The platforms talked about in the securitization chapter keep detailed records. That's what they get paid for.

Toxicity of ownership. Is the party attempting to foreclose the current holder of the properly transferred original note, properly endorsed? If not, has the document custodian been formally requested to supply this? If not, what is the purpose behind the NRM Lender not wanting to request it? Is it that the note is defective according to the pooling and servicing agreement and may be the subject of a buy-back? No lender wants to buy back a mortgage that is in default, especially when it was sold at a higher price in the form of collateralized debt obligations or credit default swaps. Is there a risk to the lender that this is not an isolated incident in the pooled mortgage trust and may expose the lender to multiple buy backs under the same circumstances? These questions and more are matters of discovering toxicity of ownership.

Toxicity can also be found in other falsified affidavits. Lenders regularly submit these to win foreclosure cases. With the proper specialist reviewing a case, they can discover and cast doubt with evidence.

Toxicity can be found in Homestead Protection. If the property's State provides homestead protection, meaning the primary residence cannot be subject to sale <u>unless</u> all owners of the property have given up the right in writing, lenders will probably require non-borrowing spouses to sign the mortgage and note, even if they are not the one to which the mortgage is being issued. This way, in a foreclosure, the bank can swoop in and evict. If discovery can show that the spouse didn't sign, or didn't receive the proper disclosures, or the signature was falsified, or the borrower does not speak English and all the documents are in English, or other evidence of impropriety, the homestead protection laws may apply. If they apply, even if the lender wins foreclosure in court, they will not be able to evict the borrower.

Toxicity can also be found in predatory lending. Take a lender, for instance, that has had its operations prosecuted against in another state. They were found guilty of predatory lending and all their loans in the state were ordered by the courts to be protected against foreclosure.

Toxicity of assignment of the mortgage. It is common to the mortgage attached to pleadings all the time, as if the mortgage and its assignment have anything to do with ownership of the debt. The mortgage is just collateral evidence of the <u>security</u> for the debt. It is <u>not</u> evidence of <u>ownership</u> of the debt. Assigning the mortgage does <u>not</u> pass <u>ownership</u> of the debt. This differentiation is Mortgage 101.

The note and mortgage together represent a negotiable instrument. Notes are assigned by endorsements properly noted at the bottom of the note of by an attachment, called an "allonge" that is stapled or otherwise "firmly attached" to the note in such a way that it becomes "a part of it".

Only the current owner of both the note and mortgage at the time the foreclosure action was begun, is the "qualified party of interest" to institute and seek the remedy of foreclosure. Anything less gives way to toxicity confirmed in State and Federal case law.

For example, Judge Burke of New York quoted several cases[34] in his LaSalle vs. Lamy decision, in pertinent part: *"well established case authorities have held that where a mortgage debt is represented by a bond or other instrument, an assignment of the mortgage without a concomitant assignment of the note or bond for which said mortgage was given as security is a nullity".*

Judge Burke goes on to say [35] "Attempting to transfer proper ownership of the note and mortgage after the case has commenced (begun) is invalid". And also in pertinent part "endorsements that have been prepared independently of the note and subsequent [after] to its execution are thus not an endorsement within the contemplation of *UCC 3-202[2]"[36].* The UCC, Uniform Commercial Code, is commonly referenced in case law and forensic mortgage analysis reports. This part of the code talks about transfers and assignments of negotiable instruments that are subject to rescission.

---

[34] *Merritt v Bartholick, 36 N.Y. 44, 34 How. Pr. 129, 1 Transc.App. 63; Flyer v Sullivan 284 A.D. 697, 134 N.Y.S.2d 521; Beak v Walts, 266 A.D. 900, 42 N.Y.S.2d 652; Manne v Carlson, 49 A.D. 276, 63 N.Y.S.2d 162, supra; Cf., Payne v Wilson, 74 N.Y. [*3] 348*

[35] Paraphrasing Judge Burke of New York in his LaSalle vs. Lamy decision.

[36] *Slutsky v Blooming Grove Inn, Inc., 147 A.D.2d 208 542 N.Y.S.2d 721, supra*

In Conclusion

Thousands of new foreclosures occur every day. Millions of foreclosures are in varying degree of process. This book was written in the hope that it would help to save many borrowers their homes from foreclosure.

Education is paramount. Borrowers as well as their advocates are in many cases, unfamiliar with the powerful weapons to fight foreclosure that were implemented by Congress and are represented by government agency regulations. Timing is critical as the most powerful remedies are governed by statutes of limitations. Waiting can only benefit the NRM Lenders at the expense of the borrowers.

Advocates defending borrowers from foreclosure need a fast, inexpensive, high quality forensic mortgage analysis service to immediately gauge violations, remedies and mortgage toxicity. They need a system that allows access from their own offices via computer, where they can engage the borrower in the process as necessary. In addition to exemplary compliance analysis and reporting, advocates require experts to be readily available to provide testimony at a reasonable fee and answer judge or opposing party concerns in the process of submitting the findings into evidence. FPG-USA provides these services.

Hopefully, the information in this book will help politicians, judges and the legal system better understand the predatory non regulated mortgage lending industry and allow them to govern accordingly. Additionally, borrowers can gain a better understanding of the challenges facing them and use this information in seeking legal representation. The loan modification professionals should use this information to effect good long term loan modification settlements, as well as help the borrower decide whether to save the home or sell it. Finally, this book was written with the belief that legal associations, associations of mortgage lenders and brokers, the real estate associations and their respective clients will all benefit from the information inside these covers.

17301886R00134

Made in the USA
Lexington, KY
03 September 2012